Permanent Wave

Dauerwelle

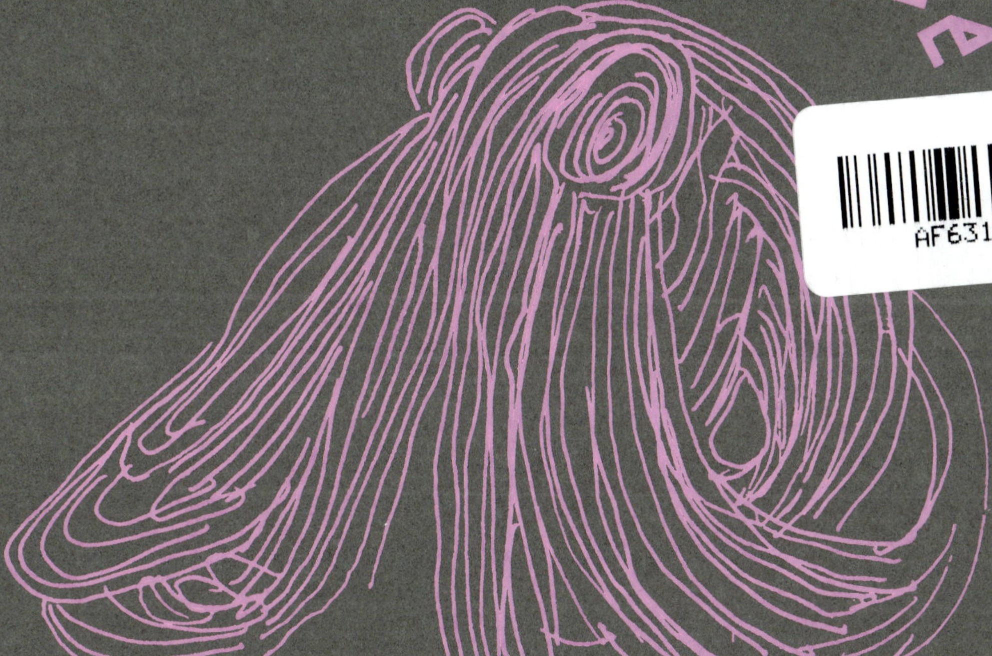

AF631967

Caroline Achaintre

Foreword Stella Rollig

Caroline Achaintre is among the leading artists of a generation, which, building on the emancipatory work of its predecessors, boasts an unquestionable mastery of all the techniques and materials suited to its themes and investigations of form. If Achaintre is described as a sculptor, it must be under the assumption that in the 2010s, sculpture can only be taken seriously as a conceptual strategy. Today, therefore, it is obviously a conceptual strategy to work with textiles and ceramics, to produce tapestries, to fire and glaze objects from hand-formed clay if, like Achaintre, the artist also makes reference to such issues as the legacy of colonialism, conceptual investigations of psychology, or the peripheries of youth culture. What is no longer necessarily very interesting is overcoming the association of textiles and ceramics with the domestic, female sphere. Female artists (and male ones) put those stereotypes to rest in the 1960s and 1970s, albeit with many setbacks and frustrations; but since the time of an epochal artist such as Rosemarie Trockel – to mention one outstanding example – with her multidisciplinary dance that transcended any prejudices against arts-and-crafts techniques, younger artists have basically been free to choose their media.

These days, a high level of interest in manual crafting processes, low-tech, and accessible materials seems to be allied to enjoyment of personal idiosyncrasies, color, and rebellion against uniform aesthetics and the stylistic imperatives of global production giants and their media cohorts. There is political potential under the surface here, or – even better – on the surface, a stubborn insistence on the value of self-empowerment, thought, and action, a joy in the confirmation of traditions, not as a shackle but as a driver of enthusiasm for what is and what can be. Achaintre's work situates her within this trend. At the same time, it seems she has been woven into an ongoing conversation with her own works that is too captivating to be interrupted, in which one word is followed by another, in which one scintillating thought gives rise to the next so that it cannot be brought to a close, although it is already well past midnight.

Vorwort Stella Rollig

Caroline Achaintre zählt zu den führenden Künstlerinnen einer Generation, die, aufbauend auf der emanzipatorischen Praxis ihrer Vorgängerinnen und Vorgänger, vorbehaltlos über alle Techniken und Materialien verfügt, die ihren Themen und Formuntersuchungen gelegen kommen. Wenn man Achaintre als Bildhauerin bezeichnet, dann unter der Voraussetzung, dass Bildhauerei in den Zehnerjahren des 21. Jahrhunderts nur als konzeptuelle Strategie ernst genommen werden kann. So ist es selbstverständlich eine konzeptuelle Strategie, heute mit Textil und Keramik zu arbeiten, Wandteppiche zu produzieren, Objekte aus handgeformtem Ton zu brennen und zu glasieren, wenn man wie Achaintre dabei, unter anderem, auf das Erbe des Kolonialismus, Begriffsuntersuchungen der Psychoanalyse oder die abgelegenen Seiten von Jugendkultur verweist. Was nicht mehr sehr zu interessieren braucht, ist die Überwindung der Konnotation von Textil und Keramik mit Sphären des Häuslichen und des Weiblichen. Mit diesen Zuschreibungen haben Künstlerinnen (und Künstler) in den 1960er-/1970er- Jahren aufgeräumt, dazumal mit vielen Rückschlägen und Frustrationen, doch spätestens seit einer epochalen Künstlerin wie Rosemarie Trockel – um eine herausragende Position zu nennen – und ihrem multidisziplinären Tanz über alle eventuellen Vorurteile gegen kunsthandwerkliche Techniken hinweg können jüngere Künstlerinnen und Künstler ihre Medien grundsätzlich frei wählen.

Gegenwärtig scheint sich starkes Interesse an handwerklichen Verfahren, Low-Tech und zugänglichen Werkstoffen mit Lust an persönlichen Idiosynkrasien, Buntheit und Widerstand gegen uniforme Ästhetiken und stilistische Imperative globaler Produktionsriesen und ihrer medialen Begleitkohorten zu verbünden. Da liegt politisches Potenzial unter oder besser an der Oberfläche, ein stures Beharren auf dem Wert von Selbstermächtigung, Denken und Tun, eine Freude an der Vergewisserung von Überlieferungen, nicht als Fußfessel, sondern als Treibriemen der Begeisterung für das, was ist und was noch kommen kann. Mit ihrer Arbeit ist Achaintre in dieser

Caroline Achaintre decided to become an artist after already having trained as a smith. Her experiences are marked by variety and opposites: having grown up in rural southern Germany, she now lives in London. After her smith apprenticeship came studies at Goldsmiths College. She never gives the impression of having planned a career in art – although she has now been granted one. This freedom of thought and action makes Achaintre an immensely attractive personality. Her work is unmistakable and thoroughly contemporary. In addition to countless group exhibitions, she has a long list of solo presentations, including some at renowned institutions such as Tate Britain, Castello di Rivoli, BALTIC, art associations in France and Germany – and now the project at the Belvedere.

We are very happy to be able to show the first solo exhibition by Caroline Achaintre in Austria, and we thank Caroline sincerely for her trust, her cooperation, and the enthusiasm with which she realized numerous new works for our project. Many thanks to Johanna Hofer, who did outstanding work as the assistant curator, and to Sibylle Reichmann and Tanja Angermann-Cekinmez for their judicious and competent handling of the production. Further thanks are due to Christian Mooney / Arcade Gallery London for loans and support.

This catalogue was wonderfully designed by Fraser Muggeridge studio, and its production was perfectly organized by Eva Lahnsteiner. Many thanks to Oriane Durand for the interview with Caroline Achaintre and to Charlotte Cosson and Emmanuelle Luciani for their essay.

Zeitströmung situiert. Und gleichzeitig scheint es, als sei sie in ein fortdauerndes Gespräch mit ihren eigenen Werken eingesponnen, das zu fesselnd ist, um es zu unterbrechen, in dem ein Wort das andere nach sich zieht, in dem ein funkelnder Gedanke einen nächsten auslöst, sodass man nicht enden kann, obwohl es schon weit nach Mitternacht ist.

Caroline Achaintre hat sich entschieden, Künstlerin zu werden, als sie bereits zur Schmiedin ausgebildet war. Vielfalt und Gegensätze prägen ihre Erfahrungen: Aufgewachsen im ländlichen Süddeutschland, lebt sie heute in London. Nach der Schmiedelehre ein Studium am Goldsmiths College. Nie vermittelt sie den Eindruck, eine Karriere im Kunstbetrieb beabsichtigt zu haben – obwohl ihr diese mittlerweile zuteilgeworden ist. Diese Freiheit des Denkens und Tuns macht Achaintre als Persönlichkeit ungemein anziehend. Ihr Werk ist unverwechselbar und ganz und gar zeitgenössisch. Neben unzähligen Ausstellungsteilnahmen ist die Liste ihrer Einzelpräsentationen lang, darunter solche in renommierten Institutionen wie Tate Britain, Castello di Rivoli, BALTIC, Kunstvereine in Frankreich und Deutschland – und nun das Projekt im Belvedere.

Wir freuen uns, dass wir die erste Einzelausstellung von Caroline Achaintre in Österreich zeigen können, und wir danken Caroline sehr herzlich für das Vertrauen, die schöne Zusammenarbeit und die Begeisterung, mit der sie zahlreiche neue Arbeiten für unser Projekt realisiert hat. Johanna Hofer hat als Assistenzkuratorin hervorragende Arbeit geleistet, vielen Dank dafür, ebenso an Sibylle Reichmann und Tanja Angermann-Cekinmez, die die Produktion umsichtig und kompetent betreut haben. Ein weiterer Dank gilt Christian Mooney / Arcade Gallery London für Leihgaben und Unterstützung.

Der Katalog wurde von Fraser Muggeridge studio wunderbar gestaltet, seine Herstellung von Eva Lahnsteiner im Belvedere Publikationsmanagement bestens geleitet. Großer Dank geht an Oriane Durand für das Interview mit Caroline Achaintre sowie an Charlotte Cosson und Emmanuelle Luciani für ihren Essay.

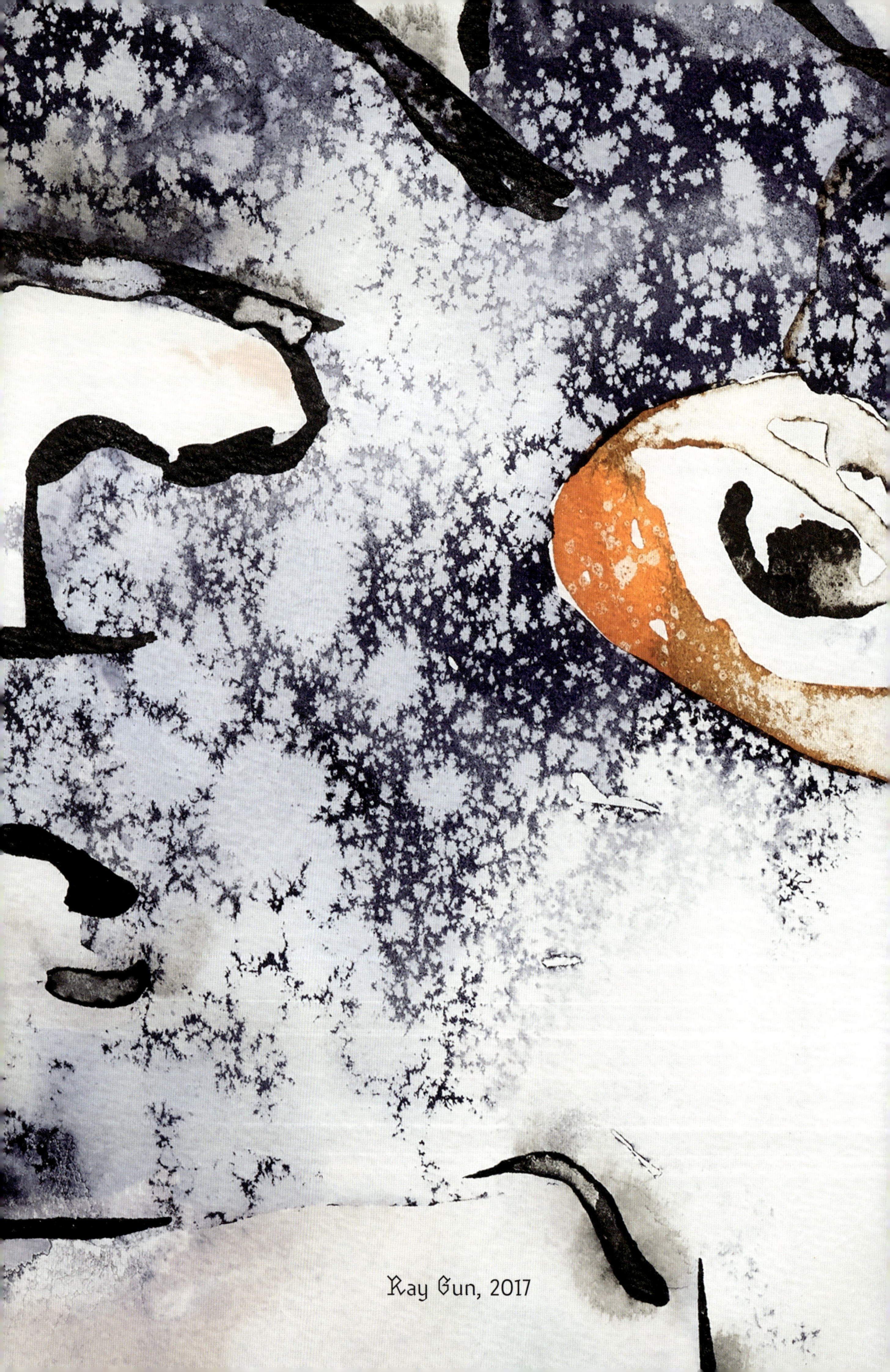

Ray Gun, 2017

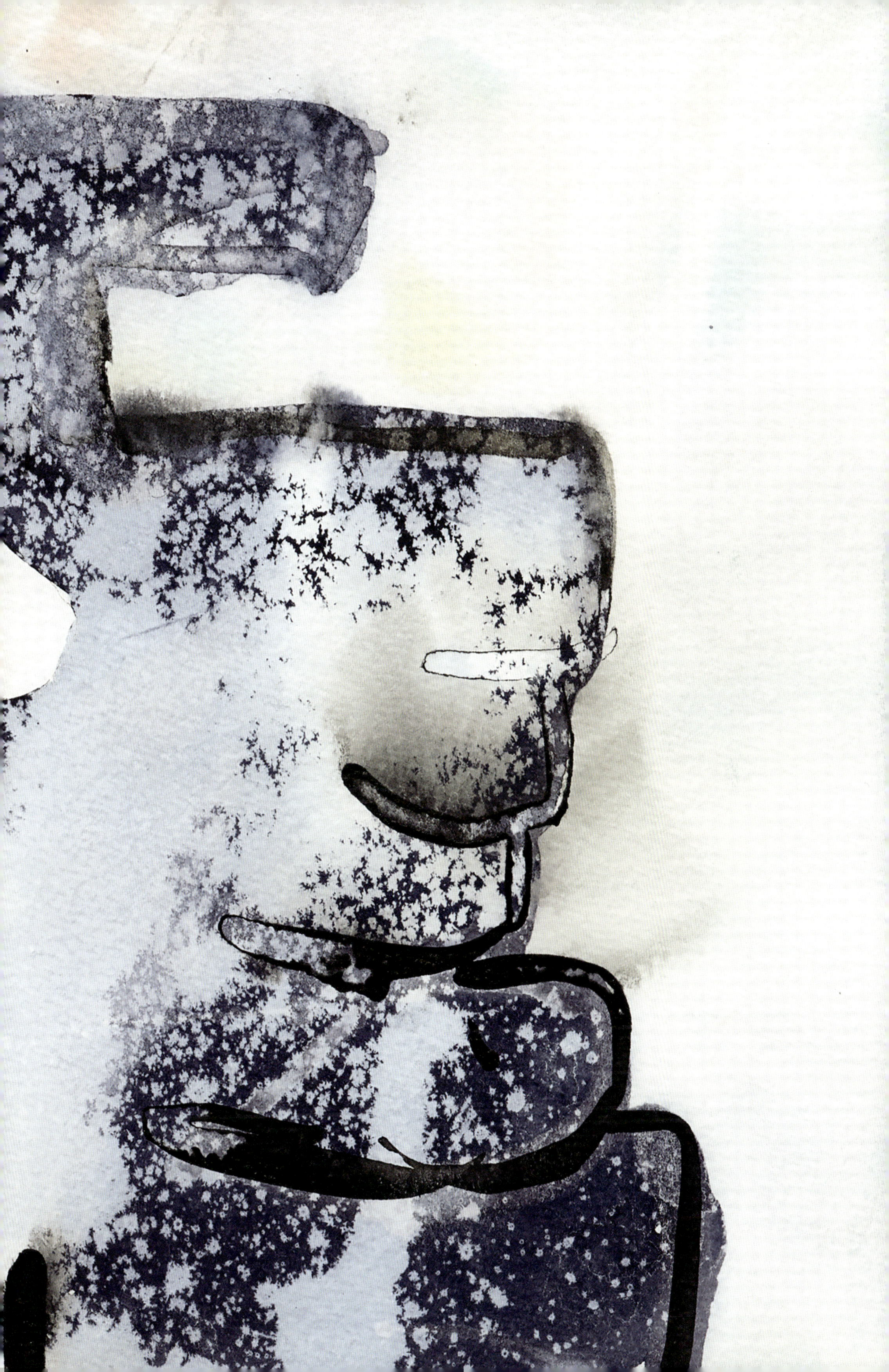

Charlotte Cosson & Emmanuelle Luciani

Caroline Achaintre: From Micro-Narratives to Macro History

Meeting with Caroline Achaintre's œuvre was like being gold diggers finding a chimp: it was the historical link bounding the youngest artists working with vernacular crafts to older ones like those from Pattern and Decoration. She was almost the only one from her generation to do so. Also, her artworks escape every attempt at categorization. We bet that each time one would like to define her work with an adjective, it would be necessary to add that her work goes beyond this very term. She is, for instance – and by far – an artist for whom notions of birth country or city of residency do not apply. Neither the fact that she is German with a French father nor that she is living in London seems to appear in her work. Where she spent her childhood, however, may have played a role in choosing to work exclusively with watercolors, ceramics, and wool. We'll come back to that particular point later on.

As often when perusing an artist's œuvre, it is particularly interesting to do so in chronological order. One will discover that Achaintre started producing works of art quite late: at the turn of the century, when she was around thirty. She indeed learned how to join, temper, weld, and hammer iron and steel before entering the Chelsea College's Art Section. Before becoming an artist, Caroline Achaintre was a blacksmith. This tension between arts and crafts – aligned with William Morris's theories before ever knowing he existed – can be felt even today.

The installation she produced in 2000 for her degree does not look like what we currently expect when entering one of her exhibitions. Far from her now familiar bestiary, this work consisted of sequins applied on a black-painted polystyrene background, forming both an old-school sound-level meter and

Charlotte Cosson & Emmanuelle Luciani

Caroline Achaintre: von Mikronarrativen zur Makrogeschichte

Als wir das Werk von Caroline Achaintre entdeckten, fühlten wir uns wie Goldgräberinnen, die einen Klumpen Gold finden: Es war ein historisches Bindeglied zwischen den jüngsten Künstlerinnen und Künstlern, die mit überlieferten Techniken arbeiten, und älteren wie den Vertreterinnen und Vertretern von Pattern and Decoration. In ihrer eigenen Generation ist Achaintre fast die Einzige, die auf diese Weise arbeitet. Aber im Grunde entziehen sich ihre Kunstwerke jedem Versuch der Kategorisierung. Wir würden wetten, dass man jedes Mal, wenn man ihr Werk mit einem Adjektiv definieren wollte, hinzufügen müsste, dass es über diesen Begriff hinausgeht. So ist sie beispielsweise eine Künstlerin, für die Vorstellungen von ihrem Geburtsland oder ihrem Wohnort völlig bedeutungslos sind. Weder die Tatsache, dass sie eine Deutsche mit einem französischen Vater ist, noch die, dass sie in London lebt, scheint in ihrem Werk sichtbar zu werden. Der Ort, an dem sie ihre Kindheit verbracht hat, könnte jedoch ihre Entscheidung beeinflusst haben, ausschließlich mit Aquarellfarben, Keramik und Wolle zu arbeiten. Auf diesen Aspekt werden wir später noch einmal zurückkommen.

Wenn man das Gesamtwerk einer Künstlerin oder eines Künstlers betrachtet, ist es oft besonders aufschlussreich, chronologisch vorzugehen. So stellt man fest, dass Caroline Achaintre erst ziemlich spät angefangen hat, Kunst zu machen: um die Jahrhundertwende, als sie ungefähr dreißig war. Bevor sie am Chelsea College of Art & Design Kunst studierte, lernte sie, wie man Eisen und Stahl zusammenfügt, härtet, schweißt und hämmert. Bevor Achaintre Künstlerin wurde, war sie Schmiedin. Diese Spannung zwischen Kunst und Handwerk – die den Theorien von William Morris entsprach, bevor sie wusste, dass es ihn gab – ist bis heute spürbar.

the word *ROCK*. Here, Caroline Achaintre's references were to be found in metal – both the music and the material. Let's unfold the allusion. At first, this installation may seem far from metalworking. However, everyone could feel the labor behind it: Achaintre obviously spent hours fixing every dot covering the wall. Her artwork is crafted: even if it is mimicking technology, it is far from being technological. A similar double bind seems at stake within the black metal songs she was constantly referring to at the time: this music arises from industrial cities – so from modernity – but also from the despair created both by industrialization and its very fall. Like rock 'n' roll, it comes from the margins, which exists in the centers, that is to say: from countercultures born within Western cities.

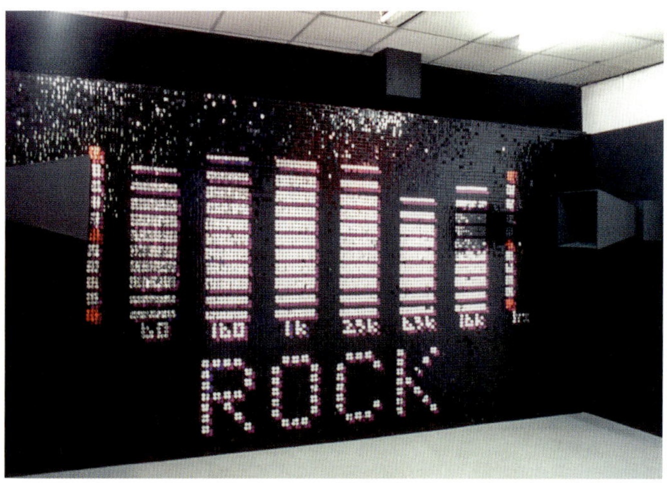

Rock, 2000

Before we continue unraveling the meaning of Caroline Achaintre's work, we'd like to be clear regarding our methodology. For us, a work of art is always a formal crystallization of either an aspect of society or of a societal change. In order to understand what it crystallized, one of our first steps is to closely look at the way those forms were produced. First, we think that if the public is so often lost when viewing contemporary art, it's because they do not understand how art production – and even production at large – shifted in the 1960s. Second, the way an object is created always reveals the value system above it. For instance, it is quite obvious that a huge, shiny, pink metal bunny, produced in a factory by dozens of assistants helped by machines before being labeled "Jeff Koons," is a perfect example of the capitalist system

Die Installation, die sie 2000 als ihre Abschlussarbeit anfertigte, sieht anders aus als das, was man heute erwartet, wenn man eine ihrer Ausstellungen betritt. Diese Arbeit, die wenig mit ihrem mittlerweile vertrauten Bestiarium zu tun hat, bestand aus Pailletten, die auf einem mit schwarzer Farbe bemalten Styroporhintergrund angebracht worden waren und einen altmodischen Schallpegelmesser und das Wort „ROCK" bildeten. Hier verwies Caroline Achaintre in zweifacher Hinsicht auf Metall – als Musikstil und als Material. Gehen wir dieser Anspielung auf den Grund: Zunächst scheint diese Installation nur wenig mit Metallbearbeitung zu tun zu haben. Dennoch war der damit verbundene Arbeitsaufwand für alle spürbar. Achaintre hatte offensichtlich Stunden damit zugebracht, alle Punkte, die die Wand bedeckten, einzeln zu fixieren. Ihr Kunstwerk ist handwerklich hergestellt: Obwohl es Technik nachahmt, ist es weit davon entfernt, selbst technologisch zu sein. Um ein ähnliches Doublebind scheint es bei den Black-Metal-Songs zu gehen, auf die sie sich damals immer wieder bezog: Diese Musik entsteht in Industriestädten – kommt also aus der Moderne – aber sie entsteht zugleich aus der Verzweiflung, die diese Industrialisierung und ihr Niedergang auslösen. Sie kommt, wie der Rock 'n' Roll, von den Rändern, die innerhalb solcher Zentren existieren, das heißt aus den Gegenkulturen, die in den Städten des Westens entstehen.

Bevor wir fortfahren, die Bedeutung von Caroline Achaintres Werk aufzudecken, möchten wir unsere eigene Methode offenlegen. Ein Kunstwerk ist für uns immer eine formale Kristallisation eines Aspekts der Gesellschaft oder eines gesellschaftlichen Wandels. Um zu verstehen, was sich in einem Kunstwerk kristallisiert hat, besteht einer unserer ersten Schritte darin, genau zu betrachten, wie seine Formen hergestellt wurden. Zum einen glauben wir, dass das Publikum so oft verwirrt ist, wenn es zeitgenössische Kunst sieht, weil es nicht versteht, wie sich die Kunstproduktion – und die Produktion ganz generell – in den 1960er – Jahren verändert hat. Zum anderen zeigt die Art und Weise, wie ein Objekt hergestellt wurde, immer, welches Wertesystem ihm zugrunde liegt. So ist beispielsweise ziemlich offensichtlich, dass ein riesiger glänzender pinkfarbener

separating ownership and labor, and its globalization in the 1980s and 1990s. We're not saying that it's bad — just that it's a typical outcome of the proud liberal system expanding at the end of the twentieth century. Following the first writings of Marx, we're thus more focused on how things are produced than on how they are received: on labor more than class struggle.[1] In the case of Caroline Achaintre's degree installation, her do-it-yourself technique of course reveals the lack of means of art students and young artists. But as she herself is still producing her works during long hours in the studio, one can say that, in a way, she embodied a new generation of people caring for handcrafted goods, local production, and workers' empowerment.

This line grew and grew as she found what is now her favorite medium: tapestry. Indeed, her work shifted from watercolors or paintings to installation, and then, when she left Goldsmiths, she dropped polystyrene to take on wool and ceramics. After 2003, she thus dropped polluting materials to take on ancestral, informed, nonneutral ones. For us, it is no coincidence that Caroline Achaintre did so after 2001. Following 9/11, everything changed: the beginning of the end of American imperialism was clear. Gravity, which is so patent in her rugs and ceramics — and which makes her forms sink toward the floor — is typical of this generation feeling the weight of History coming back the way they hadn't expected. Anyhow, this overall feeling of powerlessness or failure was already at stake in her initial rock installation, as the wall was shaken by a hidden engine. Unconsciously — as often when producing forms, and exactly how she tufted her tapestry from the back without being able to see her final patterns — she embodied what the Prix Goncourt winner Nicolas Mathieu wrote about the Nirvana generation: when they realized they couldn't make revolution anymore, all they had left was to make noise.[2]

When Caroline Achaintre turned to rug-making later in the 2000s, she also steadily made her references shift from rock to primitive. After quoting *Texas Chainsaw Massacre* or painting clownish allusions, she narrowed the gap between dark imagery

1. Karl Marx, "Estranged Labor," in *Economic and Philosophic Manuscripts of 1844*, trans. Martin Milligan (Moscow, 1959).
2. Nicolas Mathieu, *Leurs enfants après eux* (Arles, 2017).

Metallhase, der von Dutzenden Assistentinnen und Assistenten und mithilfe von Maschinen in einer Fabrik hergestellt wurde, bevor er das Label „Jeff Koons" erhielt, ein perfektes Beispiel für das kapitalistische System ist, das Besitz und Arbeit voneinander trennt und das in den 1980er- und 1990er-Jahren globalisiert wurde. Wir sagen nicht, dass dieses Kunstwerk schlecht ist – nur dass es ein typisches Resultat jenes stolzen liberalen Systems ist, das sich gegen Ende des 20. Jahrhunderts ausgebreitet hat. Im Einklang mit den frühen Schriften von Marx konzentrieren wir uns daher mehr darauf, wie Dinge hergestellt werden, als auf ihre Rezeption: mehr auf die Arbeit als auf den Klassenkampf.[1] Im Fall von Caroline Achaintres Abschlussarbeit offenbart die Do-it-yourself-Technik ihrer Installation selbstverständlich die fehlenden finanziellen Möglichkeiten von Kunststudierenden und jungen Kunstschaffenden. Doch da Achaintre ihre Werke auch weiterhin in langen Arbeitsstunden in ihrem Atelier produziert, kann man sagen, dass sie in gewisser Weise für eine neue Generation von Menschen steht, denen handwerklich gefertigte Güter, regionale Herstellung und die Ermächtigung von Arbeiterinnen und Arbeitern wichtig sind.

Dieser Trend setzte sich fort, bis sie ihr heute bevorzugtes Medium fand: Wandteppiche. Tatsächlich verlagerte sich ihre Arbeit von Aquarellen und Gemälden zu Installationen, und nachdem sie das Goldsmiths verlassen hatte, gab sie das Arbeiten mit Styropor auf und verlegte sich stattdessen auf Wolle und Keramik. Sie verzichtet also seit 2003 auf umweltschädliche Materialien und verwendet seitdem Werkstoffe, die eine lange Geschichte haben, ökologisch unbedenklich und nicht neutral sind. Es ist aus unserer Sicht kein Zufall, dass Caroline Achaintre dies nach 2001 tat. Nach dem 11. September hat sich alles verändert: Der Anfang vom Ende des amerikanischen Imperialismus war nicht zu übersehen. Die Schwerkraft, die an ihren Wandteppichen und Keramiken so deutlich sichtbar wird und die Achaintres Formen zu Boden sinken lässt, ist charakteristisch für eine Generation, die nicht damit gerechnet hatte, dass sie die Last der Geschichte noch einmal auf diese Weise spüren sollte. Jedenfalls ging es

1. Karl Marx, „Die entfremdete Arbeit" (1844), in: ders., *Ökonomisch-philosophische Manuskripte*, hg. von Barbara Zehnpfennig, Hamburg 2008, S. 54–70; www.mlwerke.de/me/me40/me40_510.htm (zuletzt besucht am 26.2.2019).

and delicate doing. The point was indeed not lying in opposition, but in reconnecting, fluidly going from one point to its seemed opposition – "staying with the trouble," as Donna Haraway would say.[3] One can perceive a path in this double change: Caroline Achaintre's work went from underlining humanity's dark side to incorporating itself within a larger perspective. Her process is inclusion-based: it creates more and more a whole. The monsters were reintegrated to characters; the masks became more and more general and nonspecific to a particular type of persona. She even reached a point where the boundary between human and animal could not be more blurred – not to mention the boundary between objecthood and aliveness.

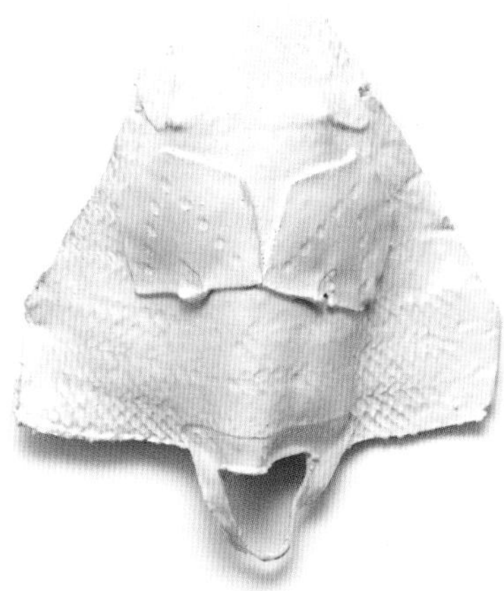

Frank, 2013

This last point may lead us to an interesting debate on shamanism and exoticism within contemporary Occidental art. Indeed, the artist claims that "it's the urge for the exotic that interests me rather than the exotic itself."[4] She is thus less interested by outside references than by humans' need to look elsewhere. Considering her works, speaking with her, we've been struck: more than underlining the colonial tastes behind the twentieth-century references or the blur between genders existing for millennia, she – again – goes beyond cultural, feminist, gender, and colonial studies by including all these stories within a bigger one. After post-structuralism and the fall of a unified past,

3. Donna Haraway, *Staying with the Trouble: Making Kin in the Chthulucene* (Durham, 2016).
4. Conversation with Caroline Achaintre, December 2017.

bereits in ihrer ersten Rock-Installation um ein umfassendes Gefühl der Ohnmacht oder des Scheiterns, da die Wand von einem verborgenen Motor erschüttert wurde. Wie so oft bei der Produktion von Formen – etwa bei der Herstellung ihrer Wandteppiche, die sie von der Rückseite tuftete, sodass sie die entstehenden Muster nicht sehen konnte – verkörperte sie unbewusst, was der Prix-Goncourt-Preisträger Nicolas Mathieu über die Generation Nirvana schrieb: Als sie erkannte, dass sie keine Revolution mehr machen konnte, blieb ihr nur noch, Lärm zu machen.[2]

Double-Dealing, 2005

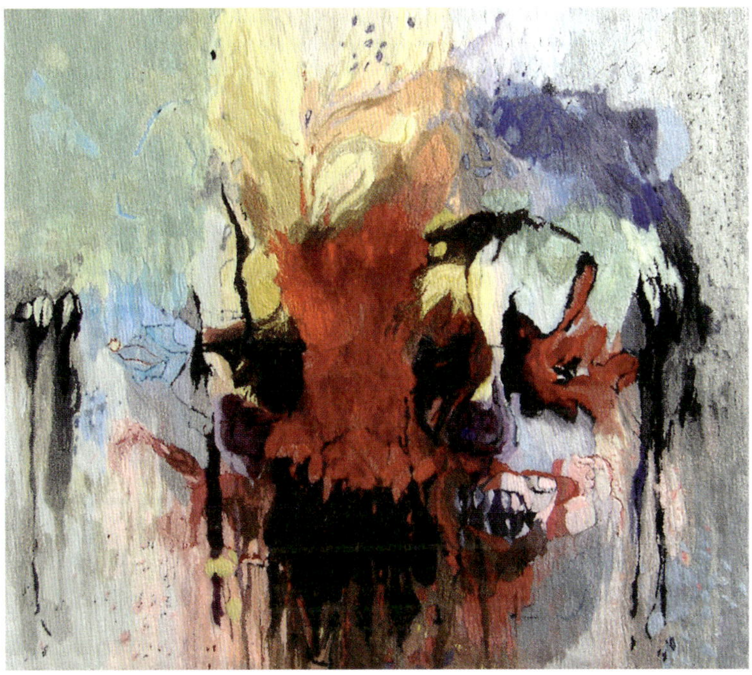

Als Caroline Achaintre in den 2000er-Jahren begann, Teppiche herzustellen, verlagerte sie ihre Referenzen zunehmend vom Rock zum Primitiven. Nach Verweisen auf *Texas Chainsaw Massacre* oder clownesken Anspielungen in ihrer Malerei verringerte sie die Kluft zwischen ihrer dunklen Bildsprache und der sensiblen Herangehensweise an die Herstellung ihrer Arbeiten. Dabei ging es weniger um Gegensätze als vielmehr um die Wiederherstellung von Verbindungen, um fließende Übergänge von einem Punkt zu seinem vermeintlichen Gegenteil – darum, „unruhig zu bleiben", wie Donna Haraway sagen würde.[3] In dieser doppelten Veränderung wird ein Weg erkennbar: Caroline Achaintres Werk

2. Nicolas Mathieu, *Leurs enfants après eux*, Arles 2017.
3. Donna Haraway, *Staying with the Trouble: Making Kin in the Chthulucene*, Durham 2016; dt.: *Unruhig bleiben. Die Verwandtschaft der Arten im Chthuluzän*, übers. von Karin Harrasser, Frankfurt am Main / New York 2018.

society needed to deepen specifically every shred of hidden, unviewed history. Now that we start to have a better view on each, it might be time to gather those to gain a bigger perspective. Caroline Achaintre is definitely Oracular / Vernacular: she participates in re-creating a unified past in order to be able to project again toward the future.[5]

We already said that a work of art is a formal crystallization of societal changes. To reveal the latter, a few steps must be followed. We talked about the first one: analyzing production. The second consists of a real art historian's job: comparing the forms newly produced with ones created in the past, and then comparing the time period in which they appeared with the one we live in — and where the forms pop up again. Last, and really not the least, this methodology needs a drop of specialization. Following Michel Serre's passe-partout metaphor,[6] one may want to dig into every knowledge field to maybe encounter the famous contemporary — and thus, to understand our time.

So why has Caroline Achaintre tufted and molded more and more animals and tribal characters? What does it says about our time? Contrary to the beginning of the twentieth century and the introduction of primitive imagery within the so-called avant-gardes, this return, contrary to a century ago, doesn't acknowledge one of the consequences of colonization. It can, though, emphasize how the world — even its farthest lands — can be touched; and the globalization of the Internet can nowadays contribute to a similar feeling. Also, the artist stresses that her tapestries get some kind of an aura, that they are charged with the energy she used to make them. This almost animistic point of view could appear to drop dead in the willfully pristine and neat GAFA (Google, Apple, Facebook, Amazon) and advertising world we live in. It would not. Firstly, as we give more and more intelligence — or, at least, room and freedom — to our everyday tools, we Occidentals are unknowingly becoming like shamans talking to nonhumans. And secondly, our dreadful time period is also the one that makes possible the encounter

5. *Oracular / Vernacular* is the project, theory, and time frame we have been developing since 2012.
6. Geneviève James, "Entretien avec Michel Serres," *The French Review*, yr. 60, no. 6 (1987), pp. 788–96.

entwickelte sich von einer Betonung der dunklen Seite der Menschheit zur Positionierung innerhalb einer umfassenderen Perspektive. Ihr Verfahren beruht auf Inklusion: Es arbeitet immer mehr darauf hin, ein Ganzes zu schaffen. Aus den Monstern wurden wieder Charaktere; die Masken wurden immer allgemeiner und unspezifischer, was bestimmte Typen von Figuren anging. Sie kam sogar an einen Punkt, an dem sich die Grenze zwischen Mensch und Tier nicht weiter verwischen ließ – von der Grenze zwischen Objekthaftigkeit und Lebendigkeit ganz zu schweigen.

Dieser letzte Punkt führt uns zu einer interessanten Debatte über Schamanismus und Exotismus in der zeitgenössischen westlichen Kunst. Tatsachlich behauptet die Künstlerin: „Das Verlangen nach dem Exotischen interessiert mich mehr als das Exotische selbst."[4] Sie interessiert sich also weniger für äußerliche Bezüge als vielmehr für das Bedürfnis von Menschen, den Blick nach außen zu richten. Bei der Beschäftigung mit ihren Arbeiten und in unseren Gesprächen mit ihr waren wir verblüfft: Achaintre betont nicht nur den Kolonialgeschmack hinter den Zitaten in der Kunst des 20. Jahrhunderts oder die seit Jahrtausenden existierende Verwischung von Gendergrenzen; vielmehr geht sie – erneut – über kulturwissenschaftliche, feministische, Gender- und kolonialgeschichtliche Untersuchungen hinaus, indem sie all diese Geschichten zu einer größeren verbindet. Nach dem Poststrukturalismus und dem Zerfall einer einheitlichen Vorstellung von der Vergangenheit entstand ein gesellschaftliches Bedürfnis, sich in jedes einzelne Bruchstück einer verborgenen, noch nicht betrachteten Geschichte zu vertiefen. Jetzt, da wir beginnen, diese Fragmente deutlicher zu erkennen, ist es vielleicht an der Zeit, sie wieder zusammenzufügen, um einen größeren Überblick zu erlangen. Caroline Achaintres Herangehensweise ist entschieden *oracular/vernacular*: Sie trägt dazu bei, eine einheitliche Vergangenheit wiederherzustellen, um sich wieder der Zukunft zuwenden zu können.[5]

Wie wir bereits erwähnt haben, ist das Kunstwerk eine formale Kristallisation des gesellschaftlichen Wandels. Um diesen Wandel

4. Gespräch mit Caroline Achaintre, Dezember 2017.
5. *Oracular/Vernacular* ist das Projekt, die Theorie und der zeitliche Rahmen, an dem wir seit 2012 arbeiten.

between the sciences and indigenous people, as quantum physics is starting to give credence to beliefs held for millennia.

A form can also appear within a need: here, the need to reconnect, both to values that exist outside of our rational time, which is reaching its end, and to the past – not to say History – in order to get a glimpse of our future. Caroline Achaintre indeed realised that what was supposed to happen in the future is almost always portrayed as primitive and what might happen usually lies in what has gone. We can go farther than Nietzsche's "return of the same"[7] and just "quote" Nature, which, with its alternation of seasons, days, and nights, follows a path where the old is always born again. Caroline Achaintre's tufted rugs are talking about a future where industrial and manual will have to coexist as much as animals and people. And it's no coincidence that her ceramics are all about presenting skins. The skin is both what protects us from one another and what allows us to be touched. How one species can touch another is one of the biggest questions the twenty-first century will have to answer.

Ray-Inn, 2010

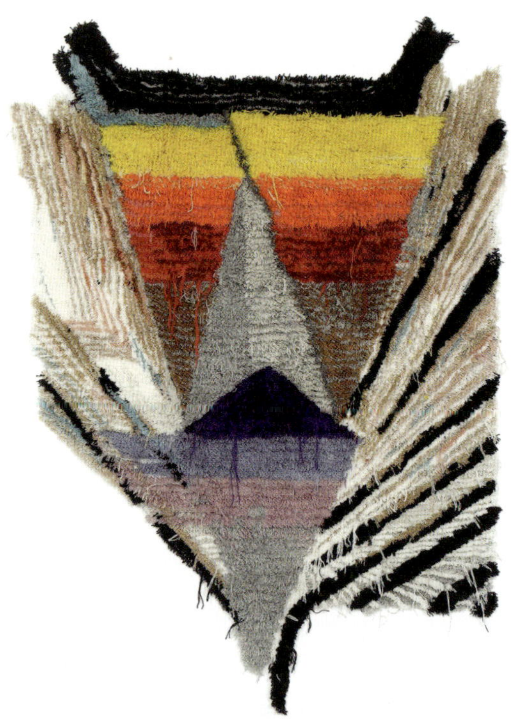

7. Friedrich Nietzsche, *The Gay Science* (Chemnitz, 1882), Aphorism #341.

offenzulegen, müssen einige Schritte befolgt werden. Über den ersten, die Analyse der Produktionsweise, haben wir bereits gesprochen. Der zweite Schritt erfordert die Arbeit echter Kunsthistorikerinnen und Kunsthistoriker: Man muss die neu entstandenen Formen mit den in der Vergangenheit geschaffenen vergleichen und dann die Epoche, in der erstere aufkamen, mit der Zeit vergleichen, in der wir heute leben – und in der diese Formen plötzlich wieder auftauchen. Und nicht zuletzt erfordert diese Methode eine gewisse Spezialisierung. Um eine allgemeingültige Metapher von Michel Serres zu verwenden,[6] kann man in jedem Wissensgebiet, das man ausgräbt, das berühmte Zeitgenössische finden – und dadurch die eigene Zeit verstehen.

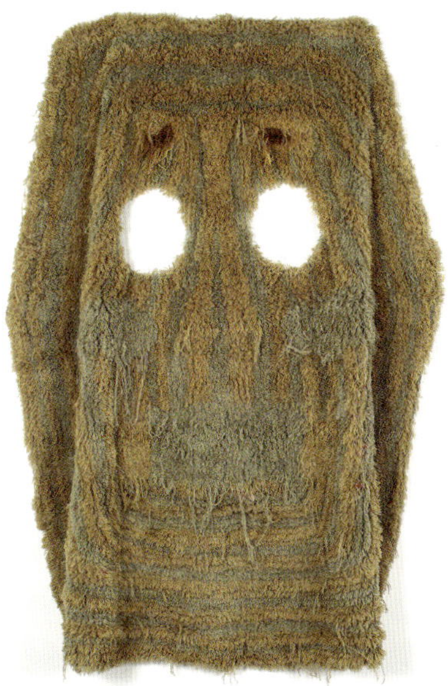

Wanderer, 2012

Warum hat Caroline Achaintre dann immer mehr Tiere und tribale Figuren getuftet und geformt? Was sagt dies über unsere Gegenwart aus? Anders als zu Beginn des 20. Jahrhunderts, als die sogenannten Avantgarden eine „primitivistische" Bildsprache einführten, würdigt Achaintres Rückgriff auf solche Formen nicht eine Folge der Kolonisierung. Doch dieser Rückgriff kann verdeutlichen, wie man mit der Welt – selbst mit den fernsten Ländern – in Berührung kommen kann; und die Globalisierung des Internets kann heutzutage ein ähnliches Gefühl auslösen.

6. Geneviève James, „Entretien avec Michel Serres", in: *The French Review*, 60. Jg., Nr. 6, 1987, S. 788–796.

Caroline Achaintre is part of an artistic family that looks at the past in order to project anew. These artists use humble, nontoxic materials and craft them with handy or vernacular techniques. In doing so, they embody a political gesture without loudly claiming it. We can trace a genealogy of these kinds of practices that would link the Nazarene painters, the Pre-Raphaelite brotherhood, Van Gogh, Giorgio Morandi, the Arte Povera, and so many others. Almost all the artists quoted here, and those working in the same vein nowadays – like Bella Hunt & DDC, Giovanni Copelli, Andrew Humke, Vincenzo Simone, etc. – come from small cities or villages like Caroline Achaintre, who grew up in a small town in southern Germany. These artists are all thinking outside of big capitals – not to say a bit outside of capitalism. It is as if they had subconsciously understood what Fredric Jameson said about capitalism's being so strong that every attempt to jump out of it will be reintegrated into the system and even form the next step to make it grow.[8] It is exactly what happens to every counterculture: what's cool and marginal always becomes the next market trend.[9] That's maybe why Achaintre dropped rock references and started to manufacture carpets: the rustic was already here when industrialization and capitalism went viral. It was already an opposite force. Lastly, the fact that she is producing rugs – one of the most domestic items – seems to go in a similar direction. Everyone, everywhere, at every time needed – and still needs – to cover the floor to live above it: it's an already globalized item. It touches everyone, everywhere, without separation.

As it arises from outside megalopolises, we call this inclination "southway."[10] It can be traced back to the eighteenth century, when medieval references first popped up. Modernity was all turned to future: progress was the viewpoint. Referencing the Middle Ages was to look at the past in a nonmodern perspective: it was even referencing precapitalist modes of producing, relating, living, and thinking. The fact that there are nowadays more and more artists who are using such medieval modes underlines that

8. Fredric Jameson, "Marxism and Postmodernism," in *The Cultural Turn: Selected Writings on the Postmodern, 1983–1998* (London, 1998), p. 40.
9. Dick Poutain and David Robbins, *Cool Rules: Anatomy of an Attitude* (London, 2000).
10. See CODE *South Way* magazine, running since 2016.

Zudem betont die Künstlerin, dass ihre Wandteppiche eine gewisse Aura bekommen und mit der Energie aufgeladen sind, die sie bei ihrer Herstellung eingesetzt hat. Man könnte meinen, dass sich eine solche fast animistische Auffassung in der gewollt makellosen und ordentlichen GAFA (Google, Apple, Facebook, Amazon) – und Werbewelt, in der wir leben, erledigt hätte. Doch das ist nicht der Fall. Erstens werden wir Menschen im Westen unbewusst zu Schamanen, die mit Nichtmenschen sprechen, indem wir die Geräte, die wir täglich nutzen, immer intelligenter machen – oder ihnen zumindest immer mehr Raum und Freiheit geben. Und zweitens ermöglicht unser schreckliches Zeitalter auch eine Begegnung von Wissenschaften und indigenen Bevölkerungen, da die Quantenphysik beginnt, jahrtausendealten Überzeugungen Glauben zu schenken.

Eine Form kann auch aus einem Bedürfnis entstehen: in diesem Fall aus dem Bedürfnis, die Verbindung zu Werten wiederherzustellen, die jenseits unseres zu Ende gehenden Zeitalters der Vernunft liegen, und eine Beziehung zur Vergangenheit – um nicht zu sagen zur Geschichte – aufzubauen, um einen flüchtigen Blick auf unsere Zukunft werfen zu können. Tatsächlich hat Caroline Achaintre erkannt, dass das, was angeblich in der Zukunft passieren soll, fast immer als „primitiv" dargestellt wird, und dass das, was passieren könnte, für gewöhnlich im bereits Vergangenen besteht. Wir können über Nietzsches „Wiederkehr des Gleichen"[7] hinausgehen und einfach die Natur „zitieren", die mit ihrem Wechsel der Jahreszeiten, Tage und Nächte einen Weg beschreitet, auf dem das Alte immer wieder neu geboren wird. Caroline Achaintres getuftete Teppiche sprechen von einer Zukunft, in der das Industrielle und das Manuelle ebenso koexistieren werden müssen wie Tiere und Menschen. Und es ist kein Zufall, dass es in ihren Keramiken immer um die Präsentation von Häuten geht. Die Haut ist das, was uns voreinander schützt und uns gleichzeitig ermöglicht, berührt zu werden. Wie eine Spezies eine andere berühren kann, ist eine der größten Fragen, die das 21. Jahrhundert beantworten müssen wird.

7. Friedrich Nietzsche, *Die fröhliche Wissenschaft*, Stuttgart 1956, S.231f., Aphorismus #341.

our society needs references lying outside of it – for example, before capitalism – to restructure itself. Caroline Achaintre herself started to make art by doing woodcuts – a typical medium from the premodern period. Finally, during modernism, rationality replaced spirituality – and the individual replaced community. However, a kind of renewed and monistic holiness glows from the work of these southway artists – and, of course, from Caroline Achaintre's works. And this even after she dropped dark metal's pseudoreligious imagery. What we can read within her artworks is that, far from the modernist man who always wants to get bigger and bigger, today, like when God still existed, some humans want to feel smaller than something again: smaller than Nature, smaller than History, but taking part of them anyhow.

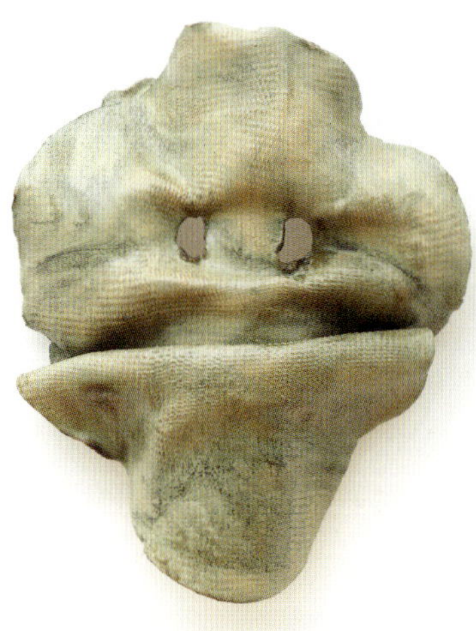

Skwash, 2014

Caroline Achaintre gehört zu einer Gruppe von Künstlerinnen und Künstlern, die auf die Vergangenheit blicken, um die Zukunft neu zu entwerfen. Sie verwenden einfache, nichttoxische Materialien und bearbeiten diese manuell in einfachen oder überlieferten Techniken. Damit verkörpern sie eine politische Geste, ohne dies laut zu verkünden. Man kann eine Genealogie solcher Praktiken zurückverfolgen, die von den Nazarenern und den Präraffaeliten über van Gogh und Giorgio Morandi bis zur Arte Povera und darüber hinaus reicht. Fast alle Genannten wie auch Künstlerinnen und Künstler, die heute ähnlich arbeiten – wie Bella Hunt & DDC, Giovanni Copelli, Andrew Humke, Vincenzo Simone und andere – kommen aus Kleinstädten oder Dörfern; so wuchs Caroline Achaintre in einem kleinen Ort in Süddeutschland auf. Diese Künstlerinnen und Künstler denken außerhalb der großen Kapitalen – um nicht zu sagen außerhalb des Kapitalismus. Es ist, als hätten sie unbewusst verstanden, was Fredric Jameson über den Kapitalismus sagte: Er ist so stark, dass jeder Versuch, aus ihm auszusteigen, wieder in das System integriert und sogar den nächsten Schritt bilden wird, der sein Wachstum fördert.[8] Genau das passiert mit jeder Gegenkultur: Was cool und randständig ist, wird immer zum nächsten Markttrend.[9] Vielleicht hat Achaintre deshalb die Rock-Zitate aufgegeben und begonnen, manuell Teppiche herzustellen. Das Ländliche war schon da, als sich die Industrialisierung und der Kapitalismus mit großer Geschwindigkeit ausbreiteten. Es war bereits eine Gegenkraft. Letztlich scheint die Tatsache, dass *Achaintre* Teppiche – besonders stark mit Häuslichkeit konnotierte Gegenstände – herstellt, in eine ähnliche Richtung zu weisen. Die Menschen mussten überall und immer schon den Boden bedecken, um darauf zu leben, und sie müssen es immer noch: Der Teppich ist ein immer schon globalisierter Gegenstand. Er berührt alle, überall, ohne Trennungen.

Da diese Tendenz außerhalb von Megastädten entstanden ist, nennen wir sie „South Way".[10] Sie lässt sich zurückverfolgen bis ins 18. Jahrhundert, als zum ersten Mal Rückbezüge auf das

8. Fredric Jameson, „Marxism and Postmodernism", in: ders., *The Cultural Turn: Selected Writings on the Postmodern, 1983–1998*, London 1998, S. 40.
9. Dick Pountain/David Robbins, *Cool Rules: Anatomy of an Attitude*, London 2000.
10. Siehe die Zeitschrift *CODE South Way*, die seit 2016 erscheint.

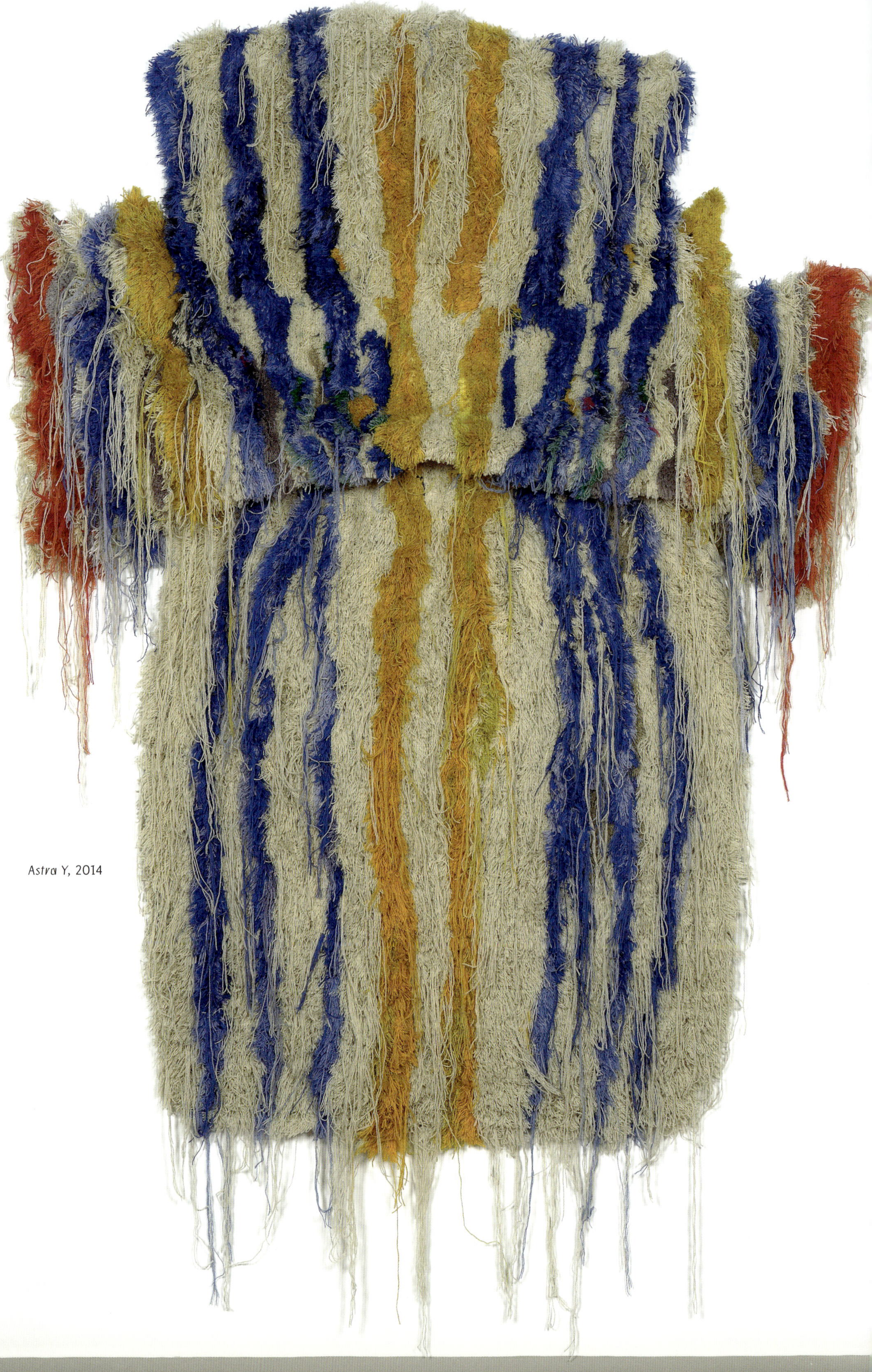

Astra Y, 2014

Mittelalter aufkamen. Die Moderne war ganz auf die Zukunft ausgerichtet: Ihr Gesichtspunkt war der Fortschritt. Auf das Mittelalter zu verweisen bedeutete, die Vergangenheit von einem nichtmodernen Standpunkt zu betrachten und sich sogar auf präkapitalistische Formen des Produzierens, Erzählens, Lebens und Denkens zu beziehen. Die Tatsache, dass sich heute immer mehr Kunstschaffende solcher mittelalterlicher Verfahren bedienen, verdeutlicht, dass unsere Gesellschaft für ihren Umbau Bezugspunkte braucht, die außerhalb von ihr – also beispielsweise vor dem Kapitalismus – liegen. Caroline Achaintre selbst begann ihre Kunstproduktion mit der Herstellung von Holzschnitten – einem typischen Medium der Vormoderne. Schließlich trat in der Moderne die Rationalität an die Stelle der Spiritualität – und das Individuum an die Stelle der Gemeinschaft. Doch in den Arbeiten der Künstlerinnen und Künstler des „South Way" glüht eine neuartige, monistische Heiligkeit. Das gilt selbstverständlich auch für die Arbeiten von Caroline Achaintre – auch dann noch, als sie die pseudoreligiöse Bildsprache des Dark Metal aufgegeben hatte. An ihren Kunstwerken können wir erkennen, dass sich manche Menschen heute – anders als der Mensch der Moderne, der immer größer werden will – wieder kleiner fühlen möchten, so wie damals, als Gott noch existierte: kleiner als die Natur, kleiner als die Geschichte, aber trotzdem als ein Teil von ihnen.

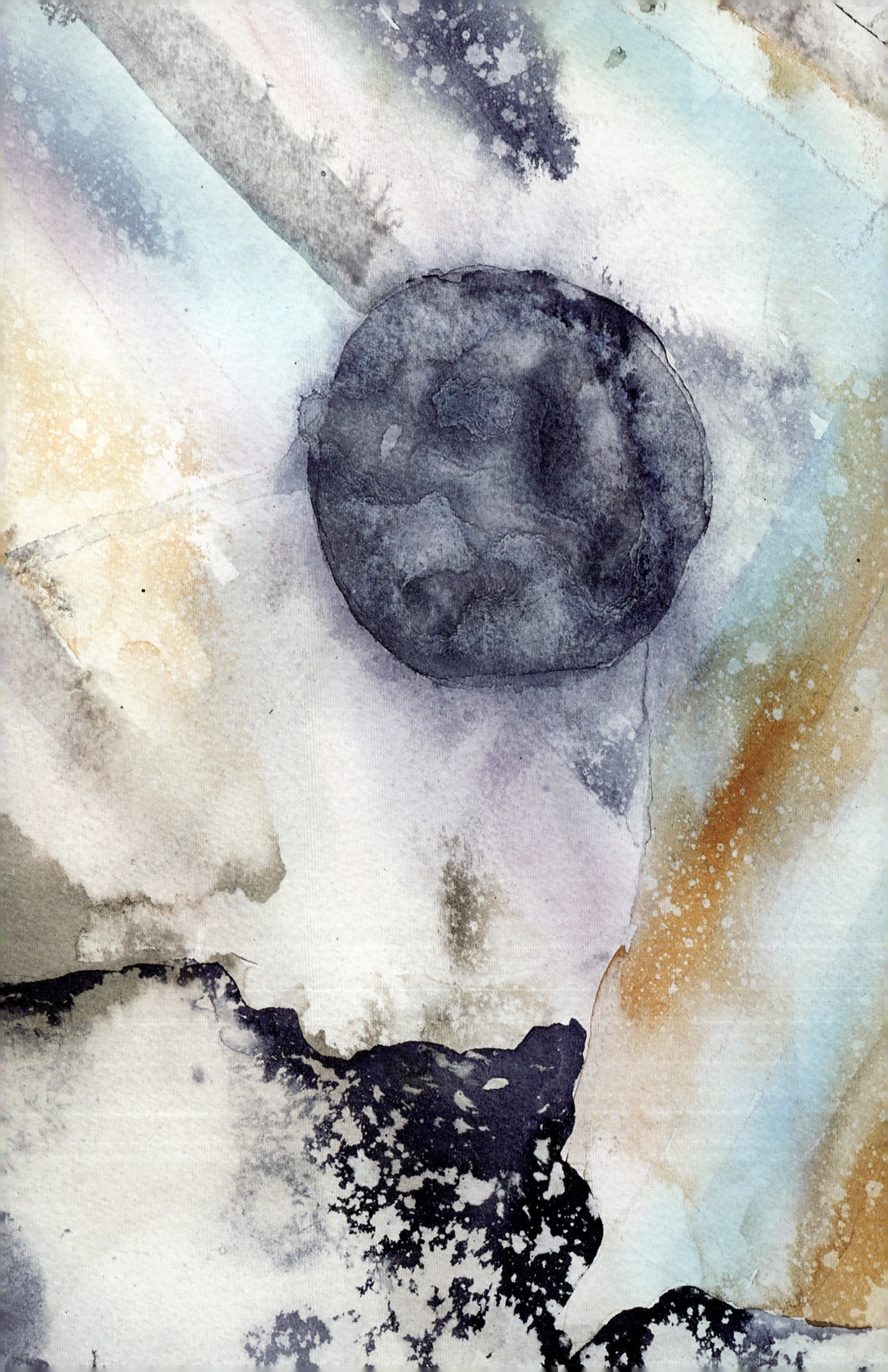

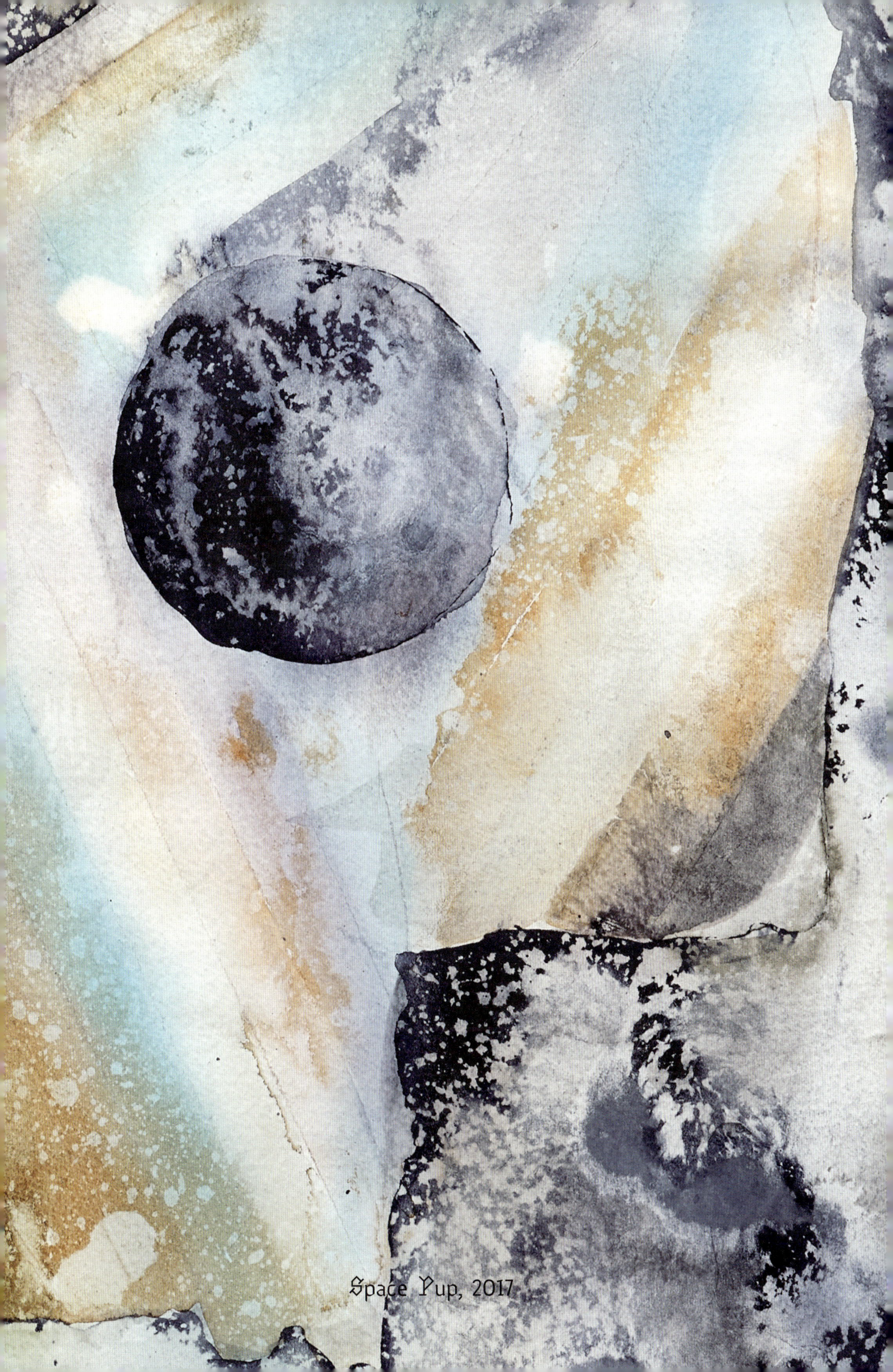

Space Pup, 2017

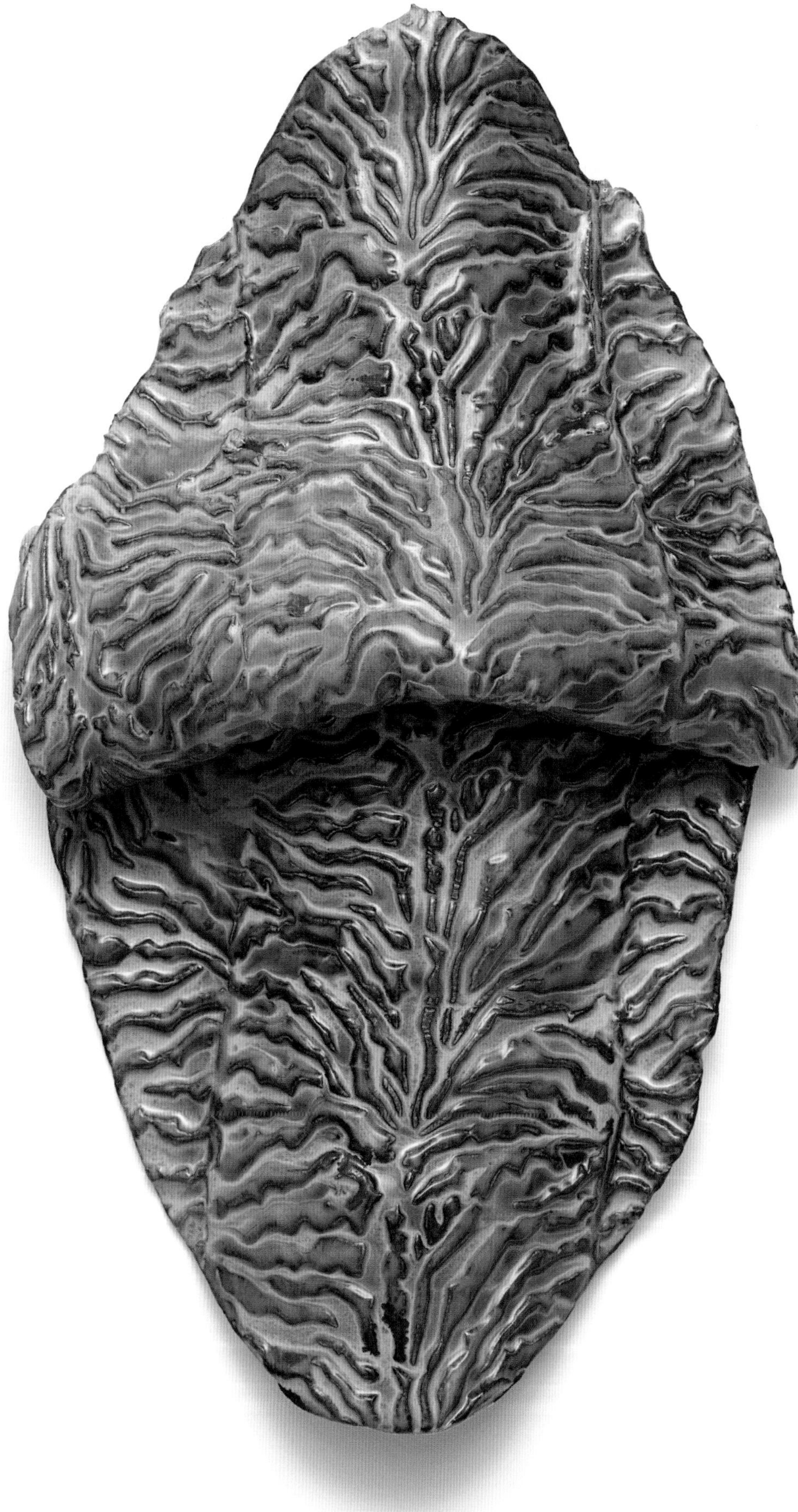

Licker, 2019

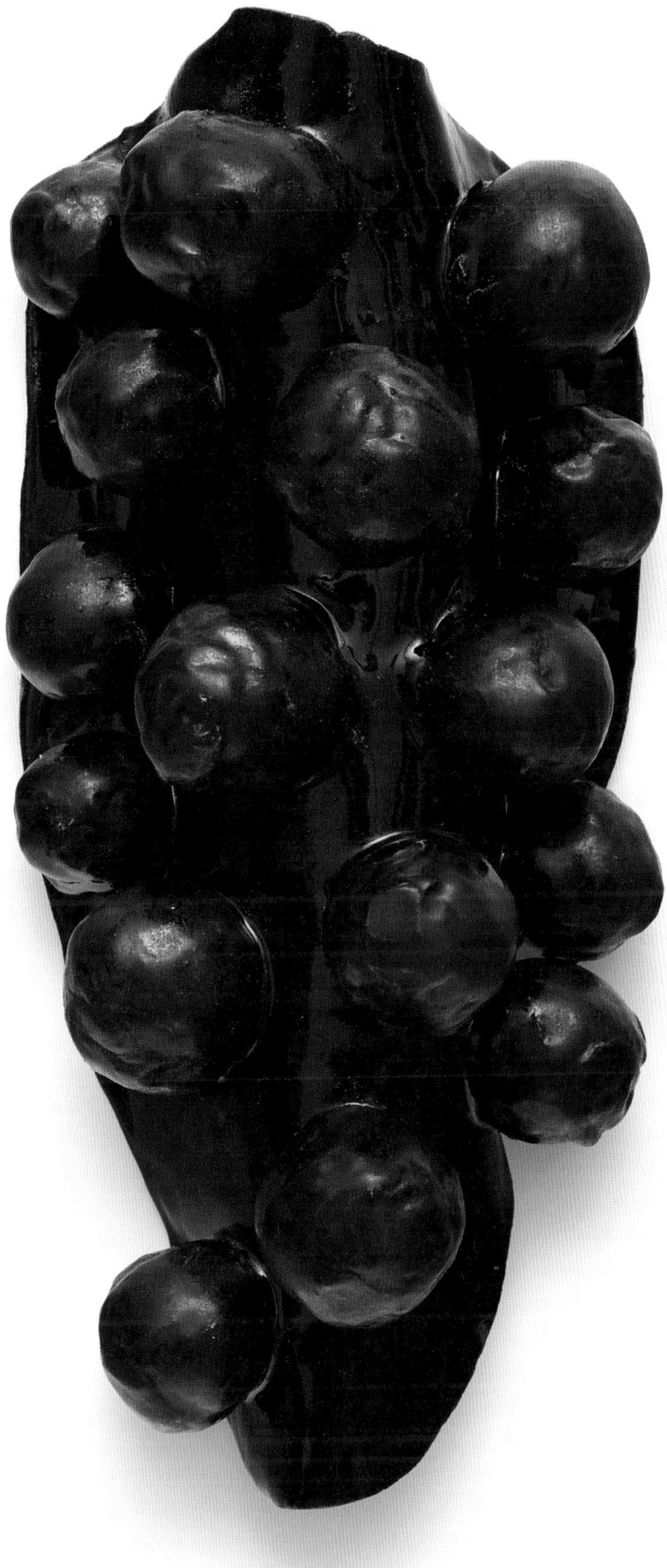

Re-Wine, 2019

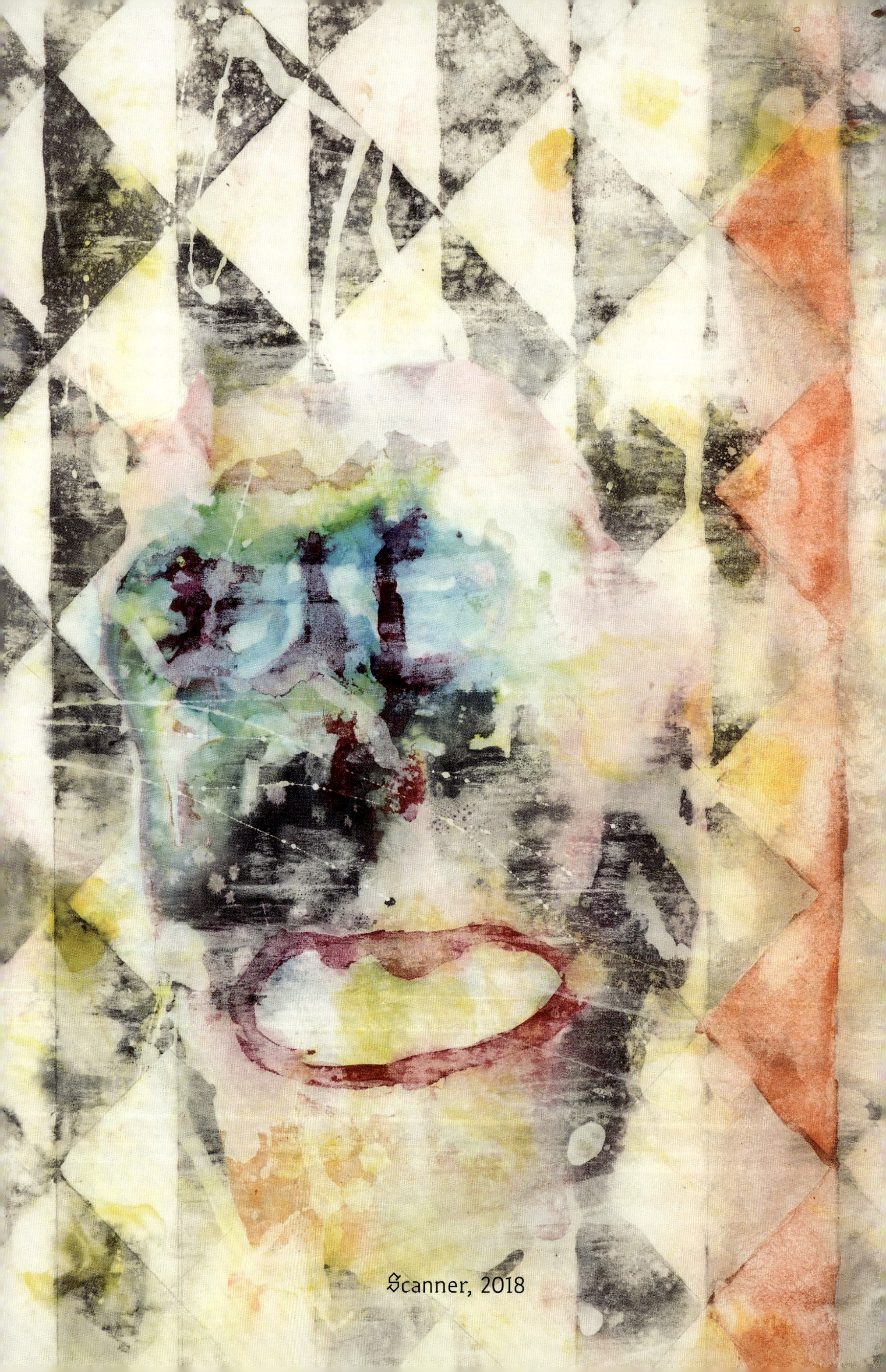

Scanner, 2018

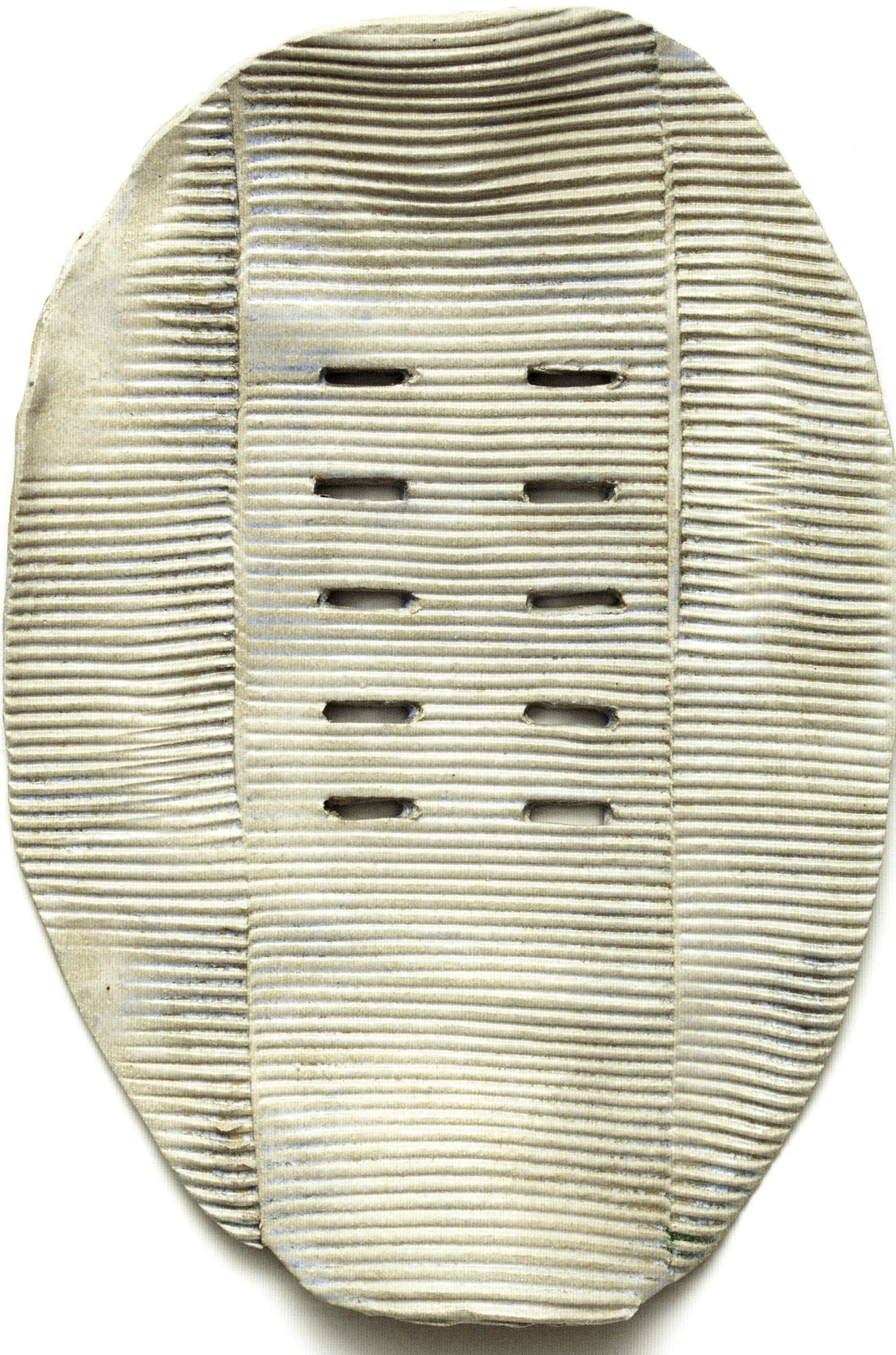

Tenpence, 2019

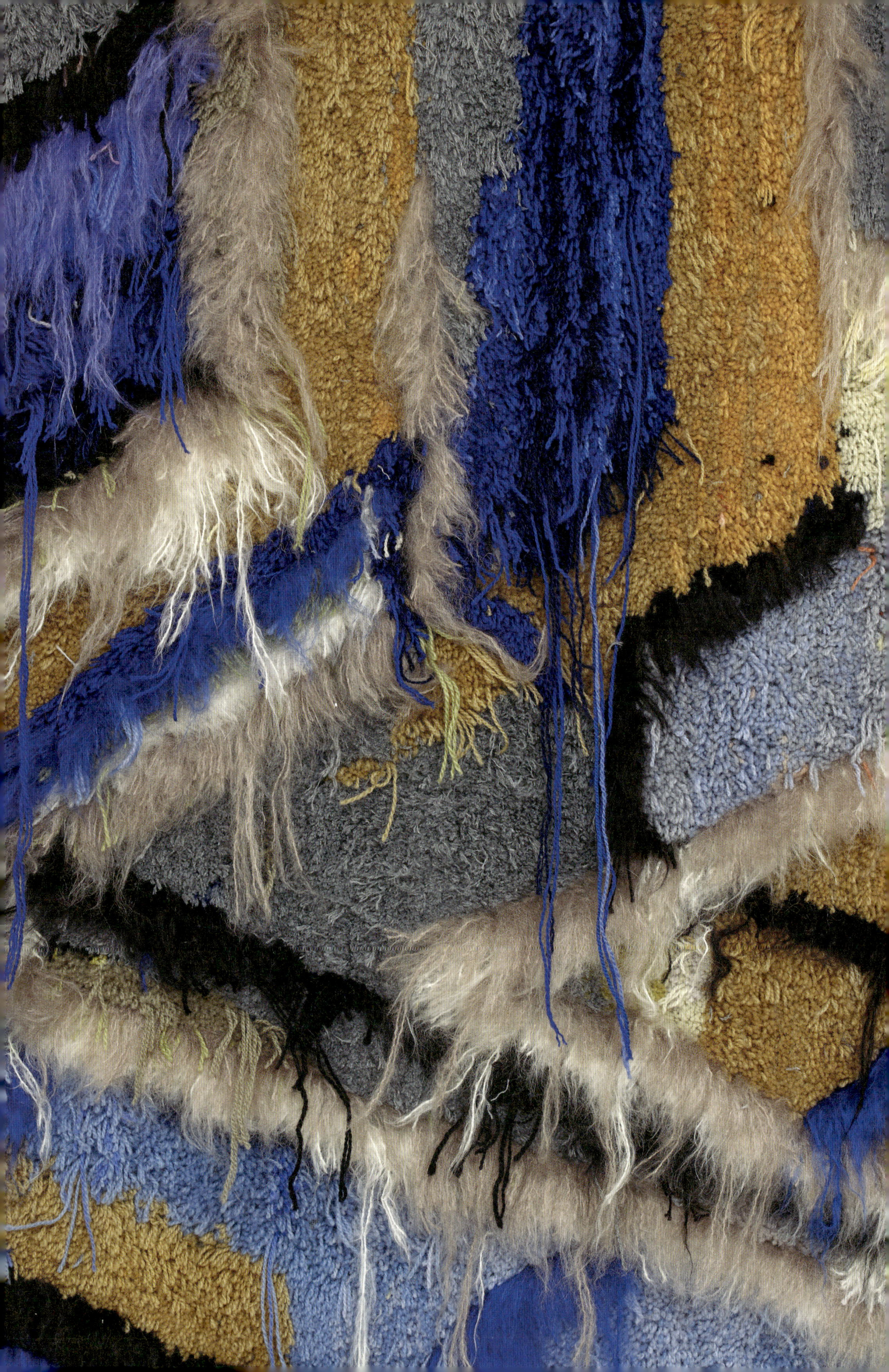

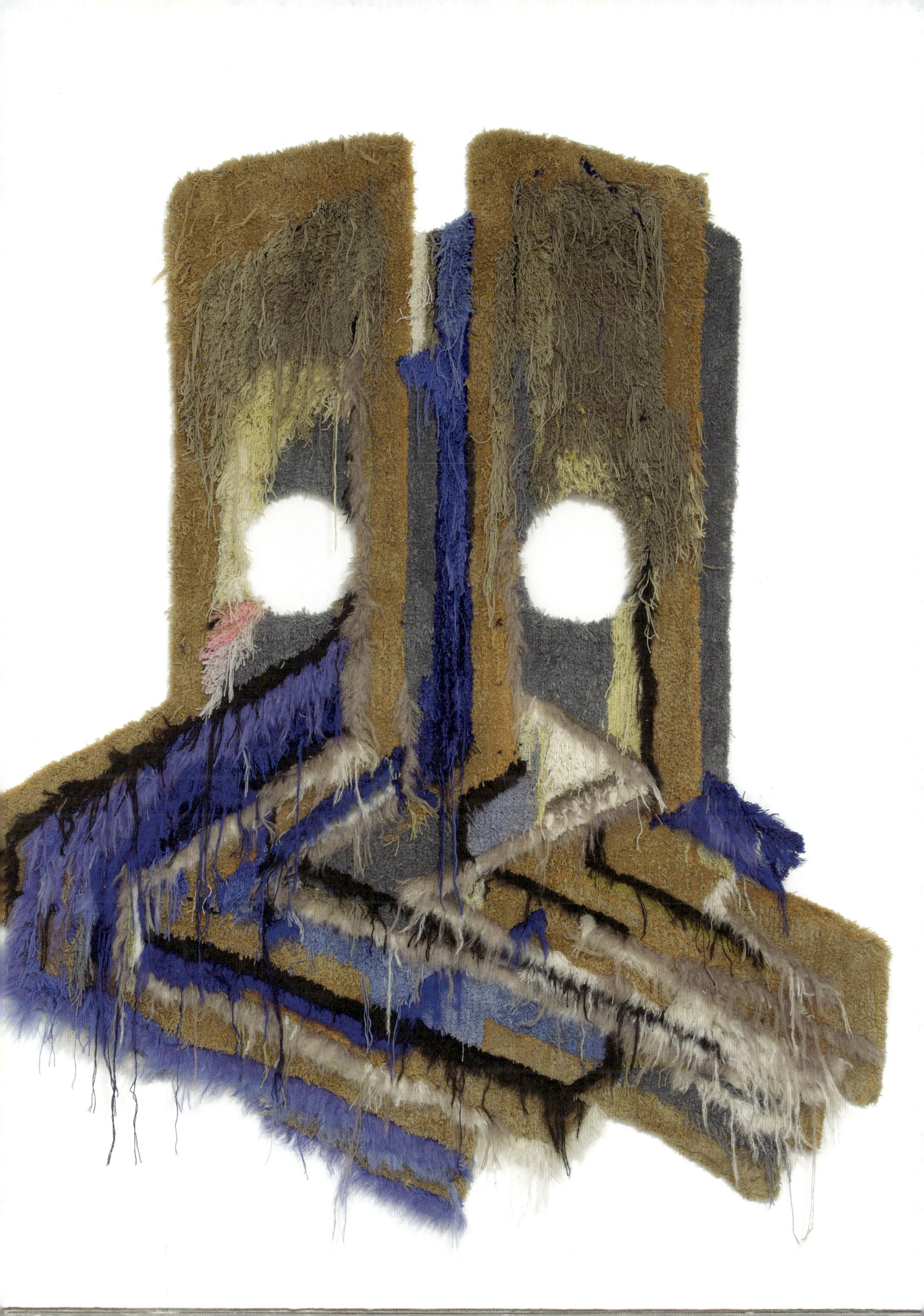

Cruizer, 2019

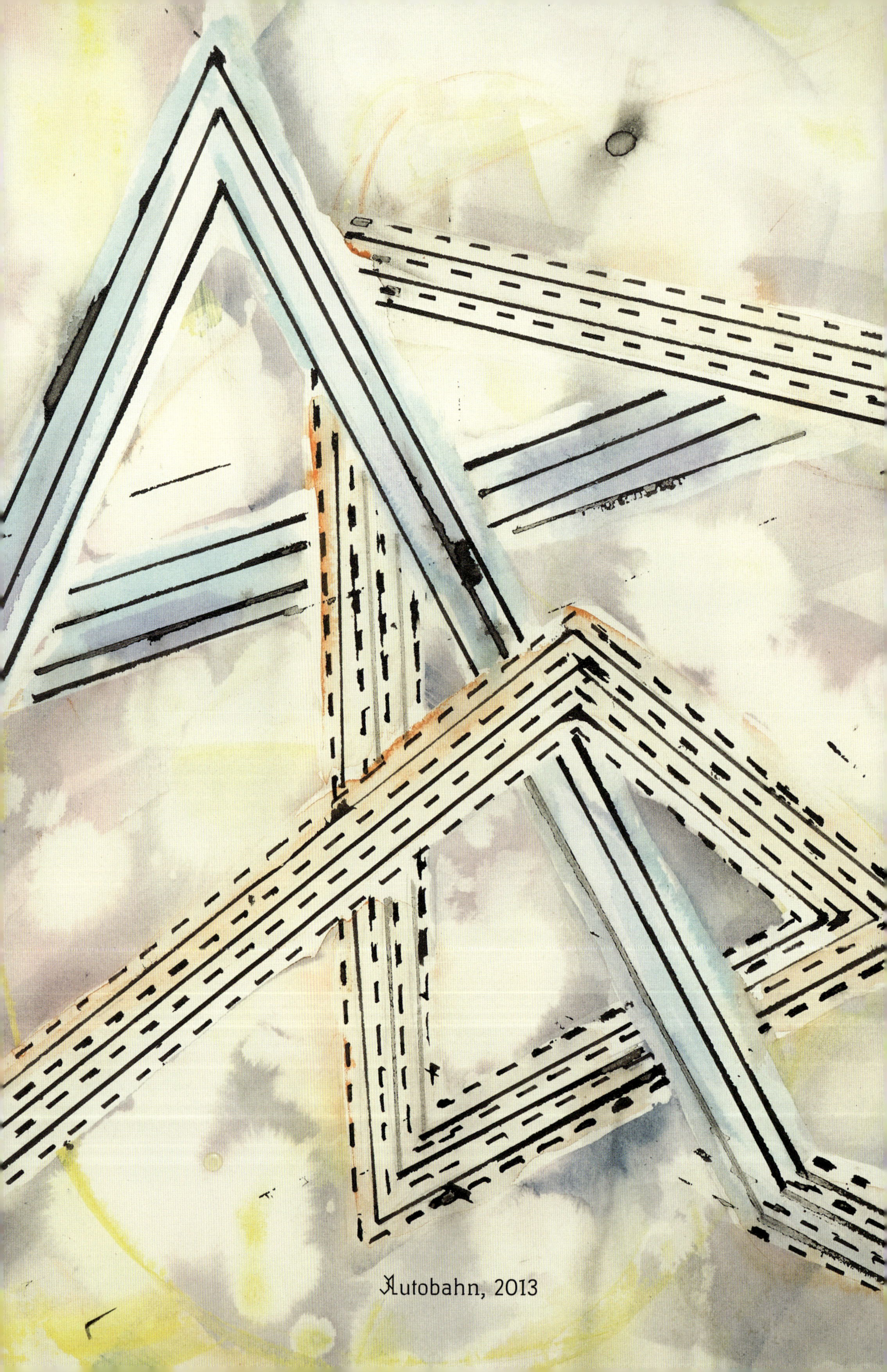

Autobahn, 2013

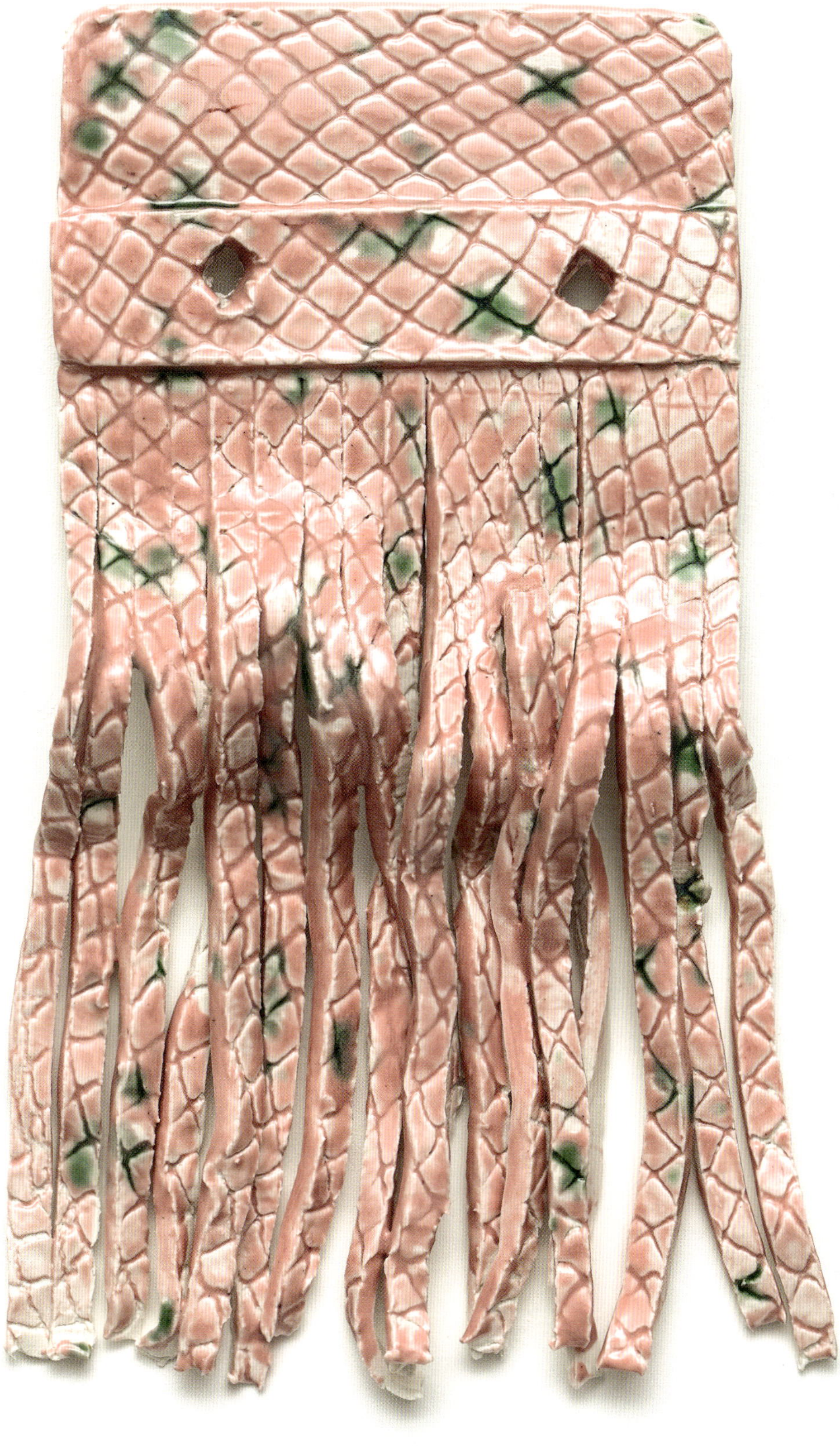

El Duster, 2019

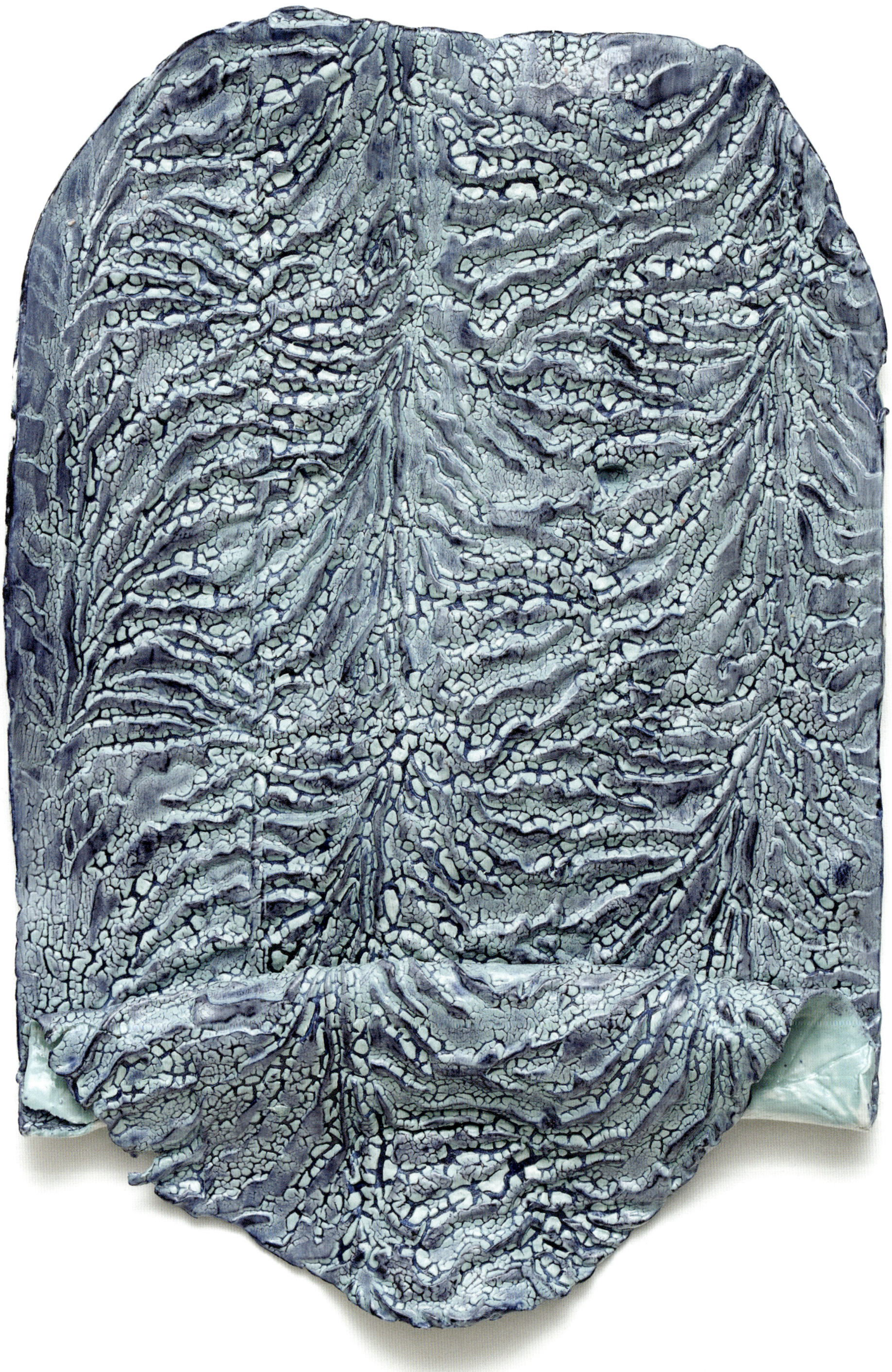

Tatter, 2019

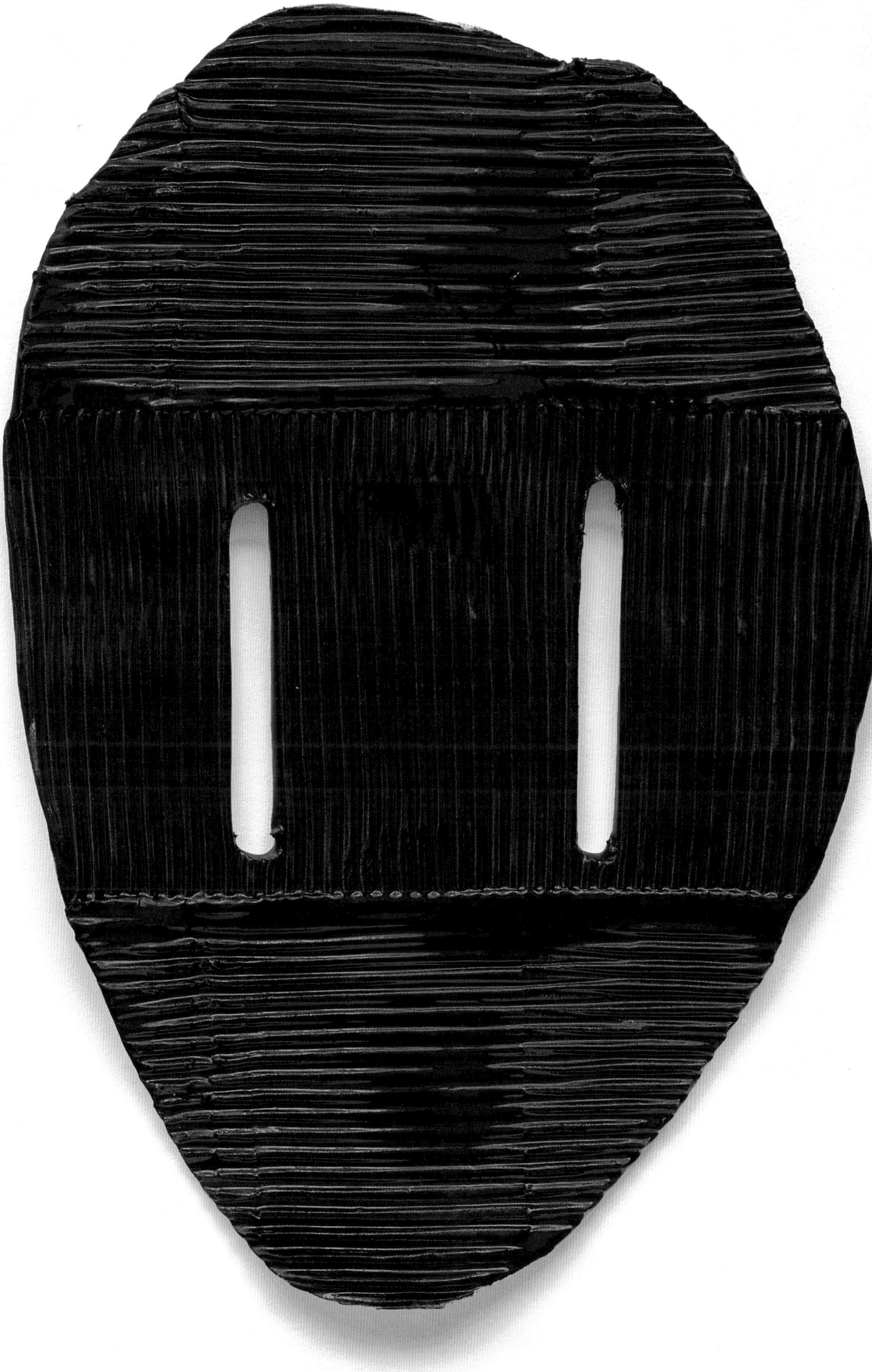

Monika, 2019

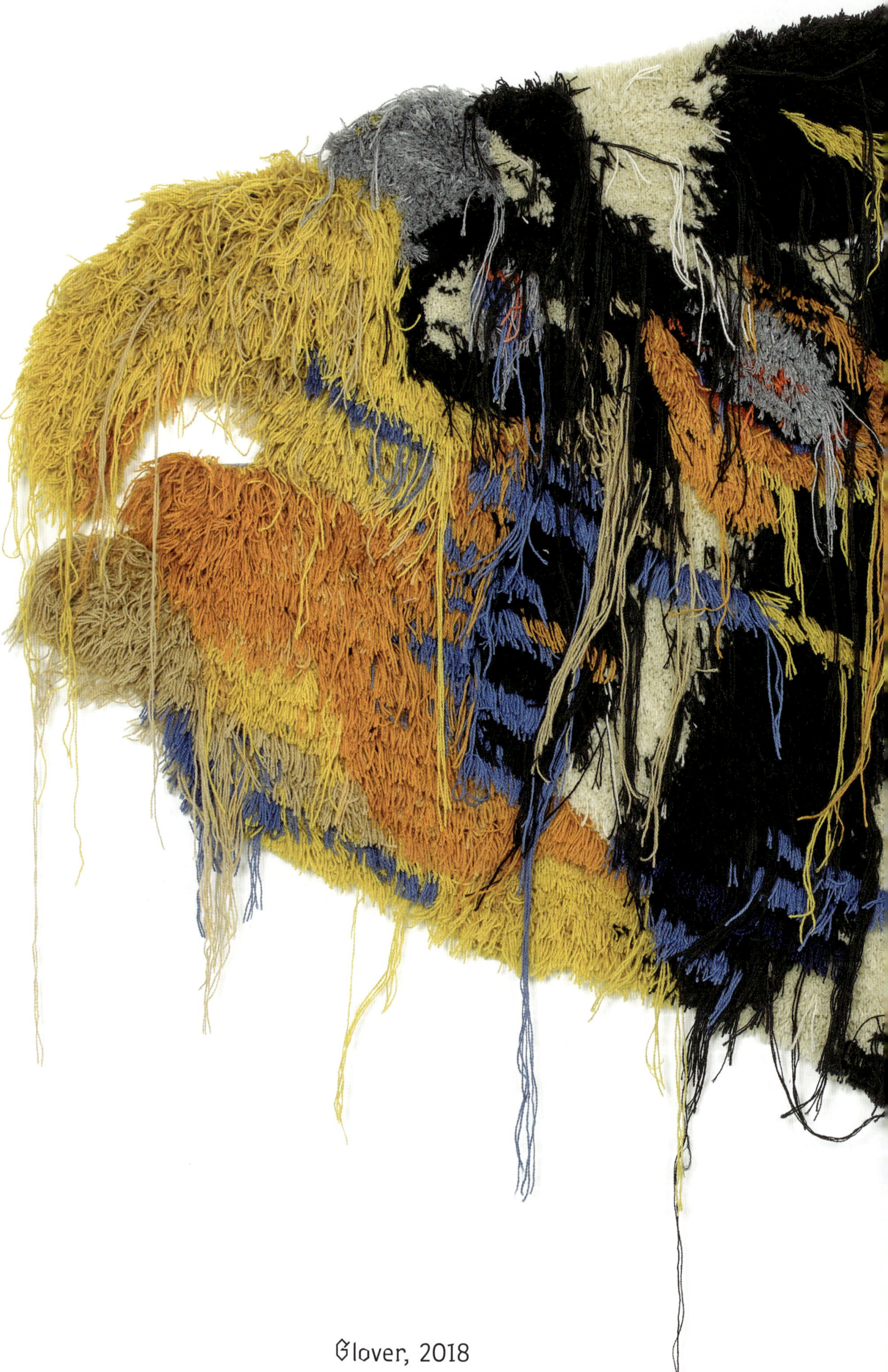

Glover, 2018

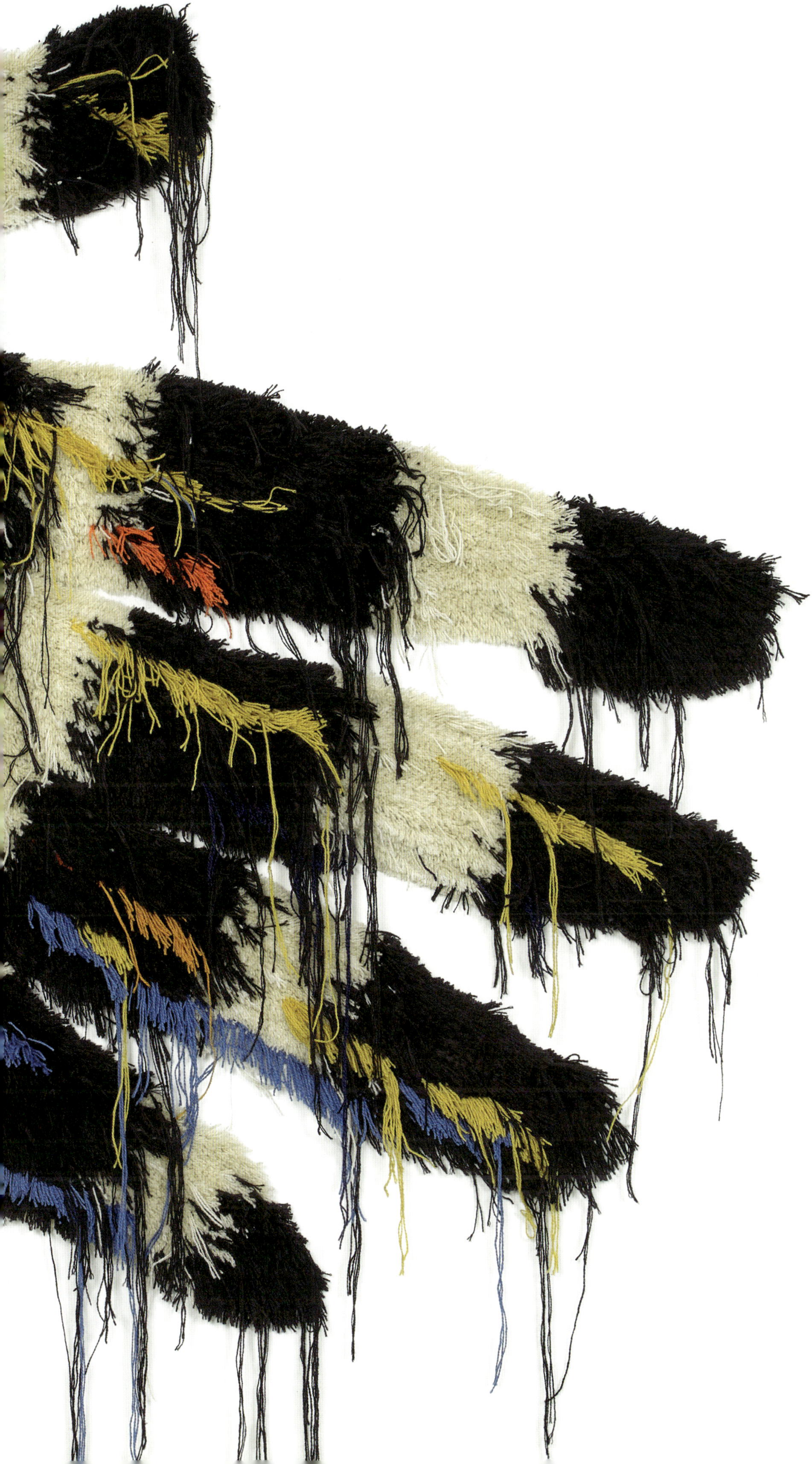

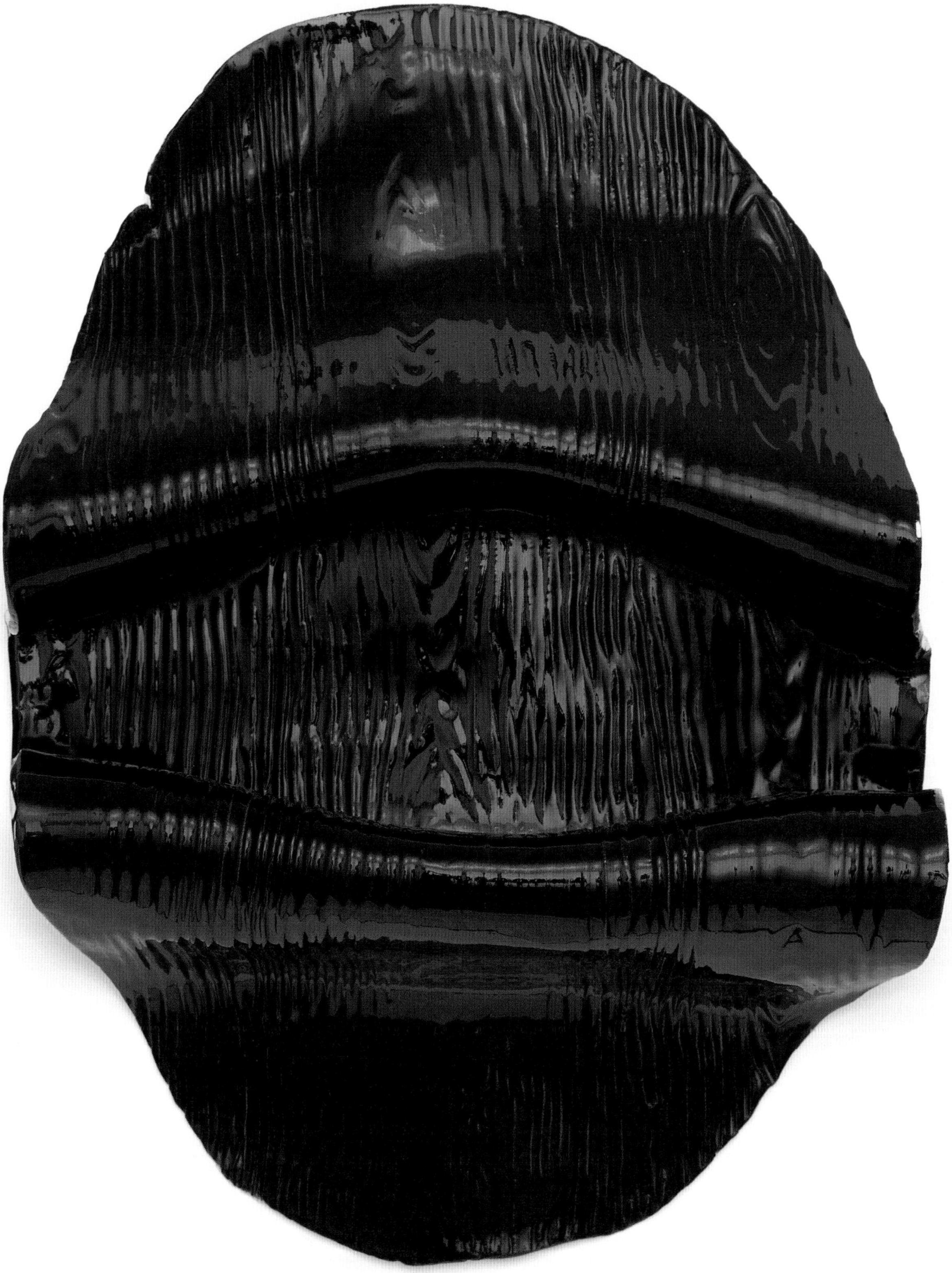

Ernest, 2019

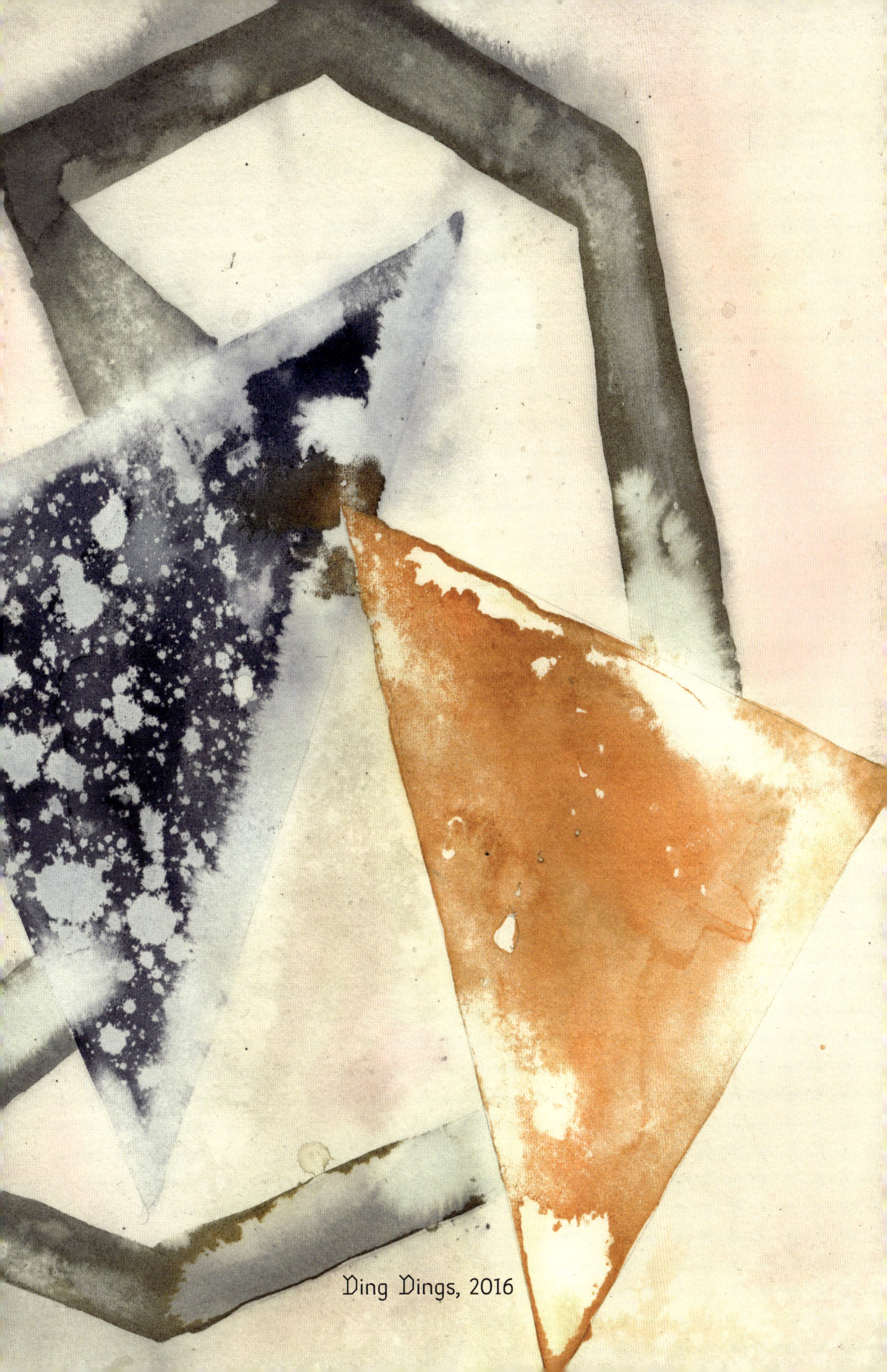

Ding Dings, 2016

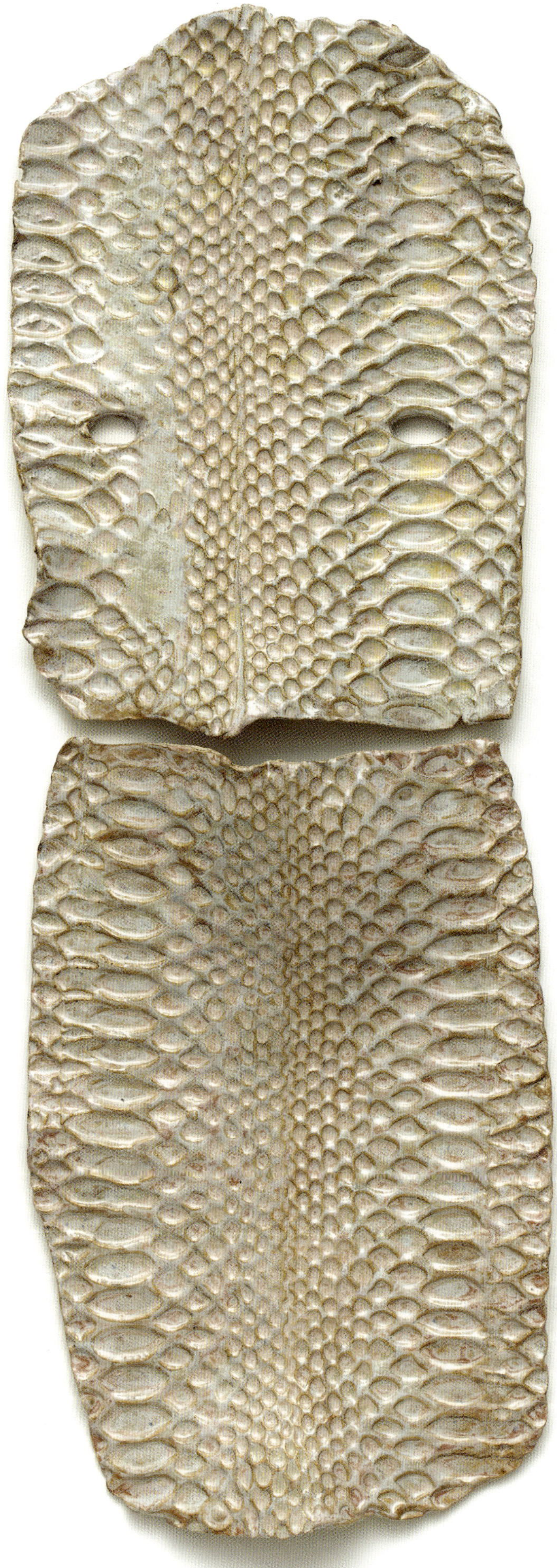

Sir Plus, 2019

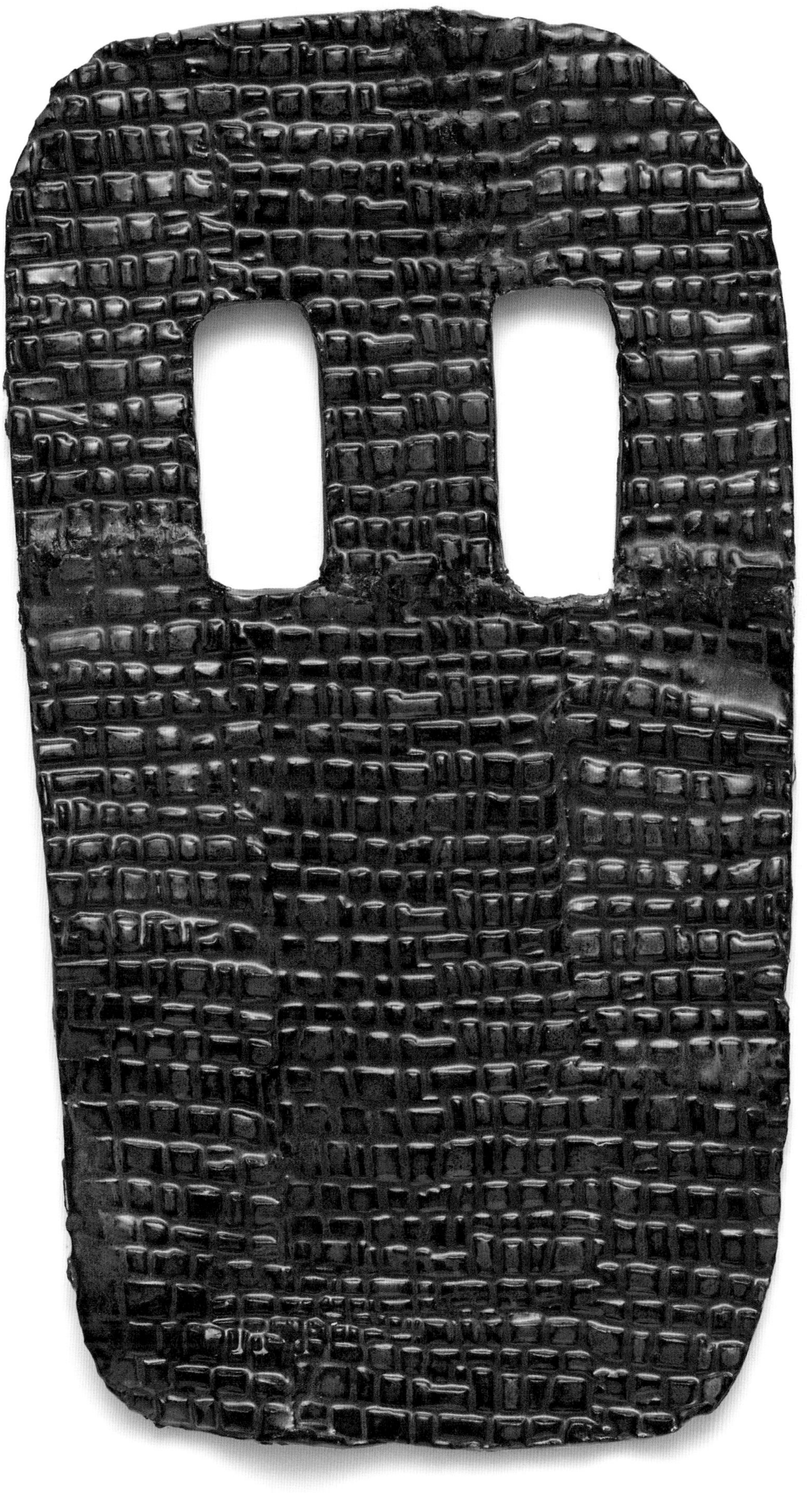

Ashlar, 2019

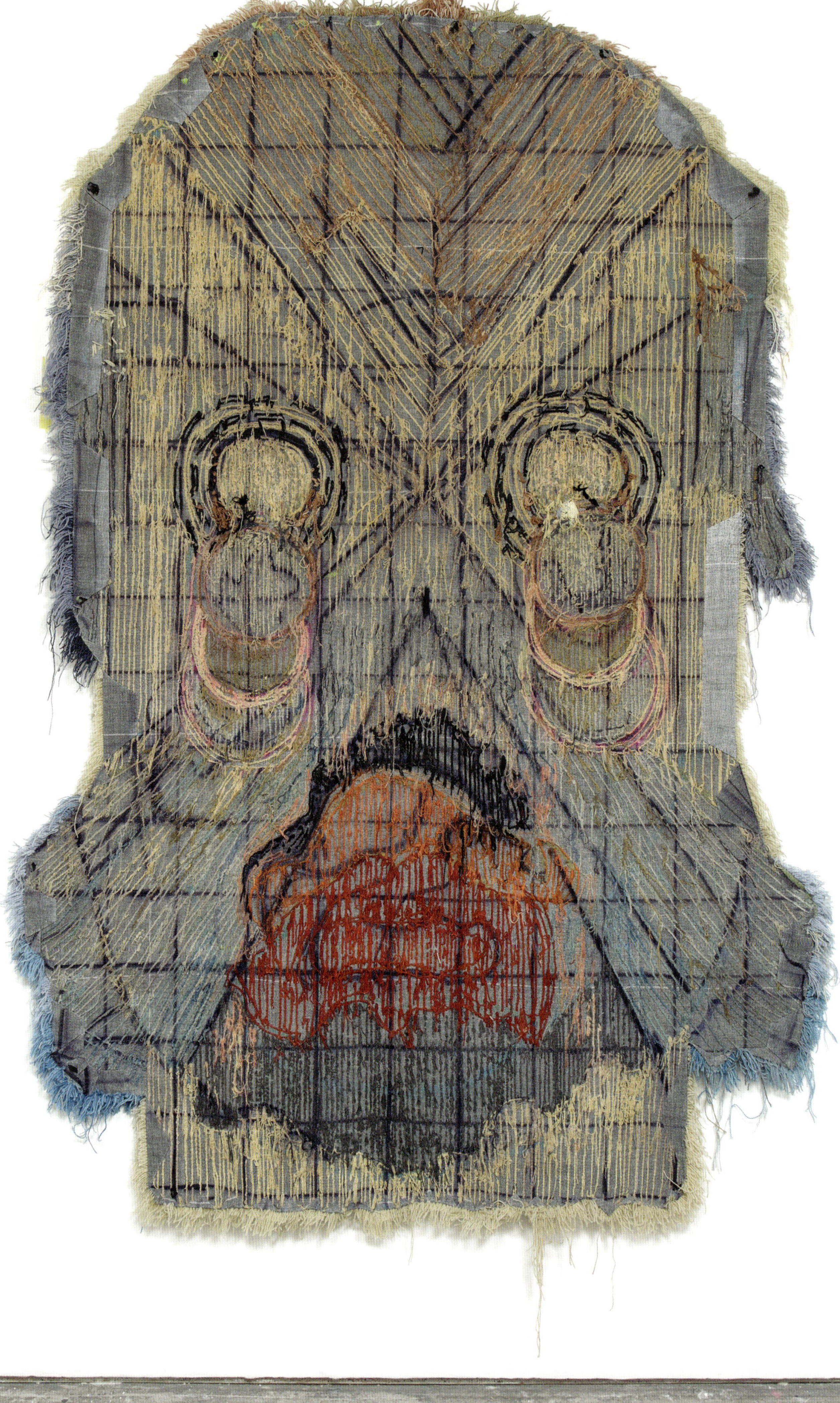

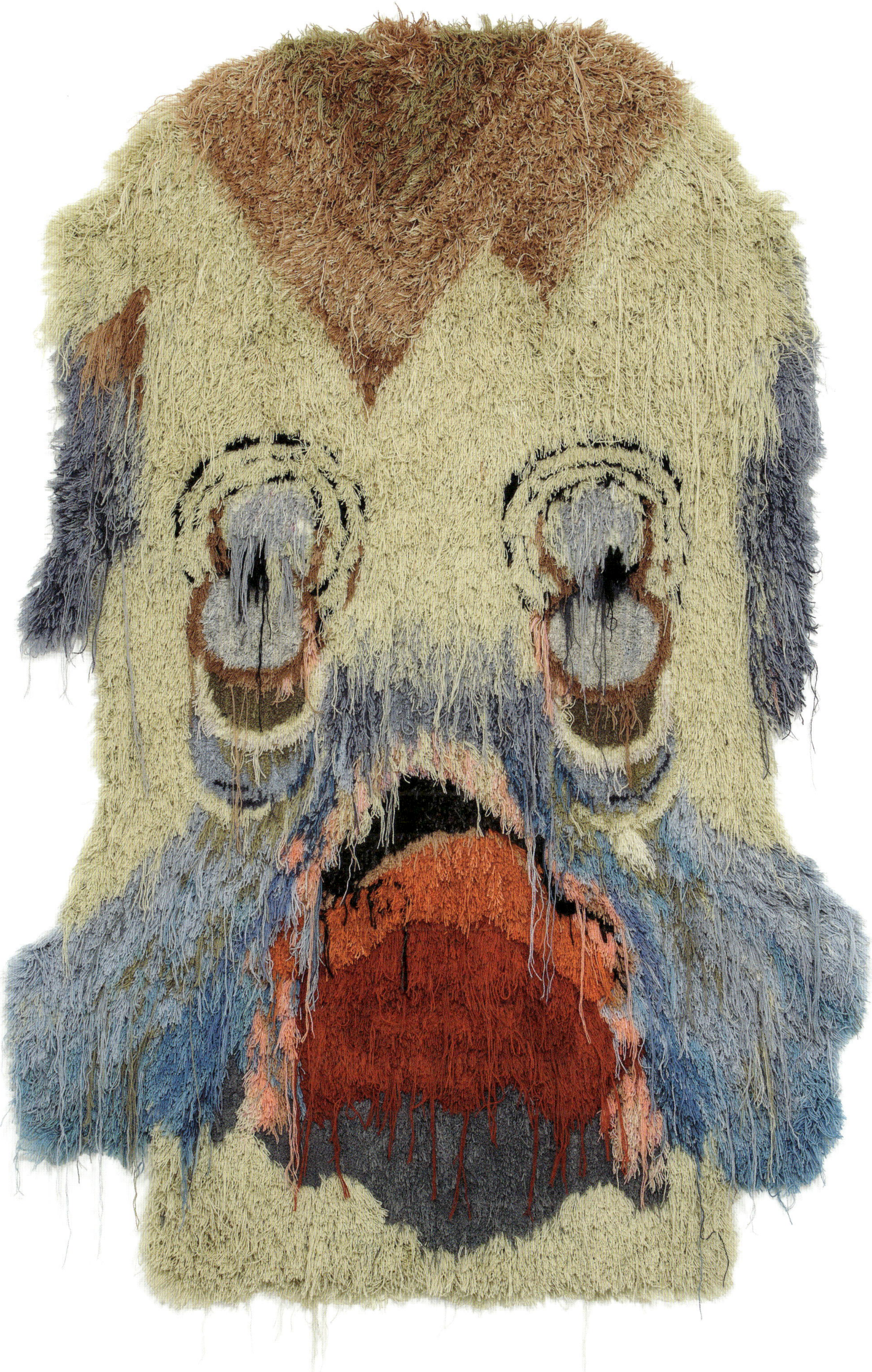

Brunco, 2019

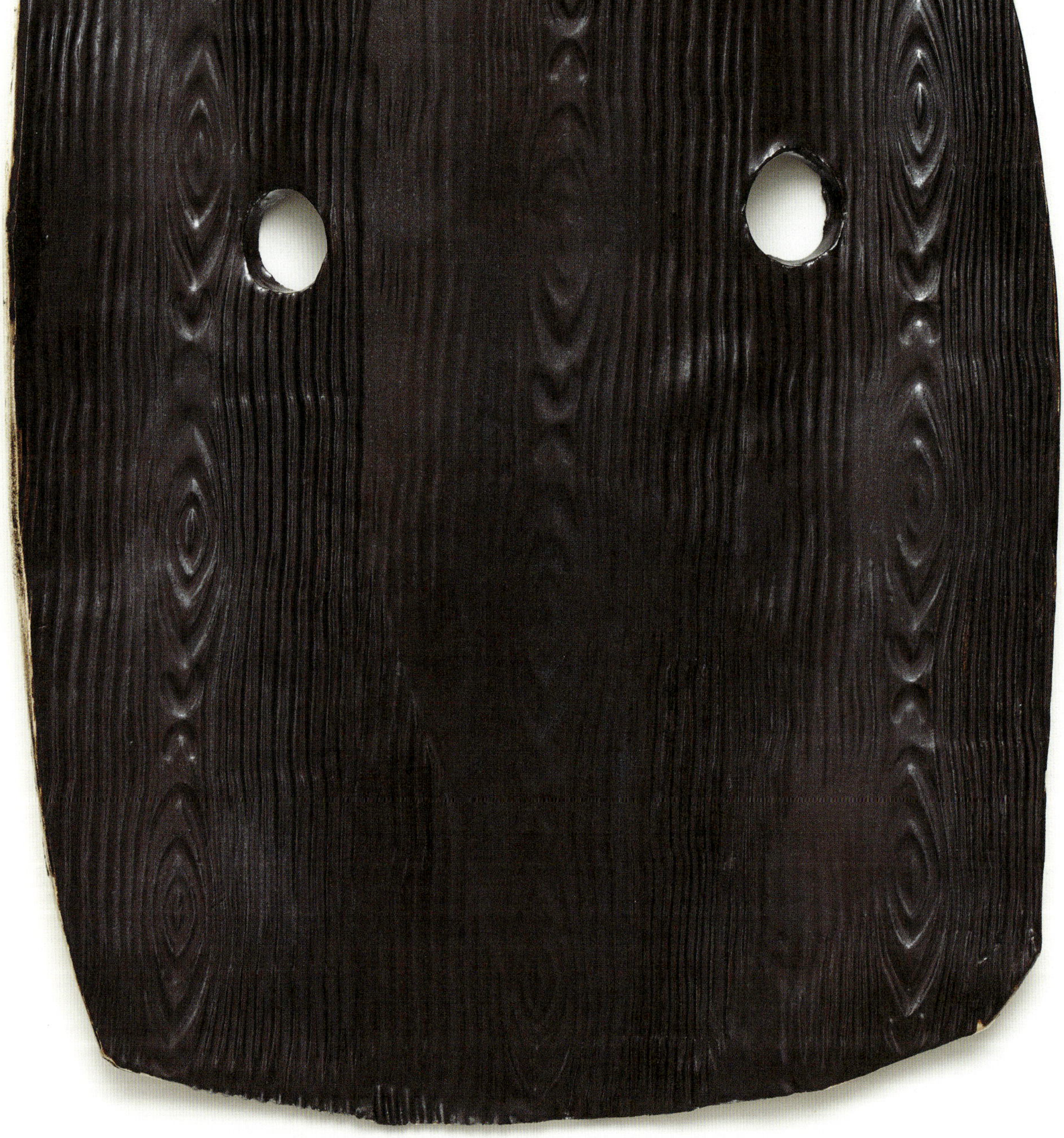

Borg, 2019

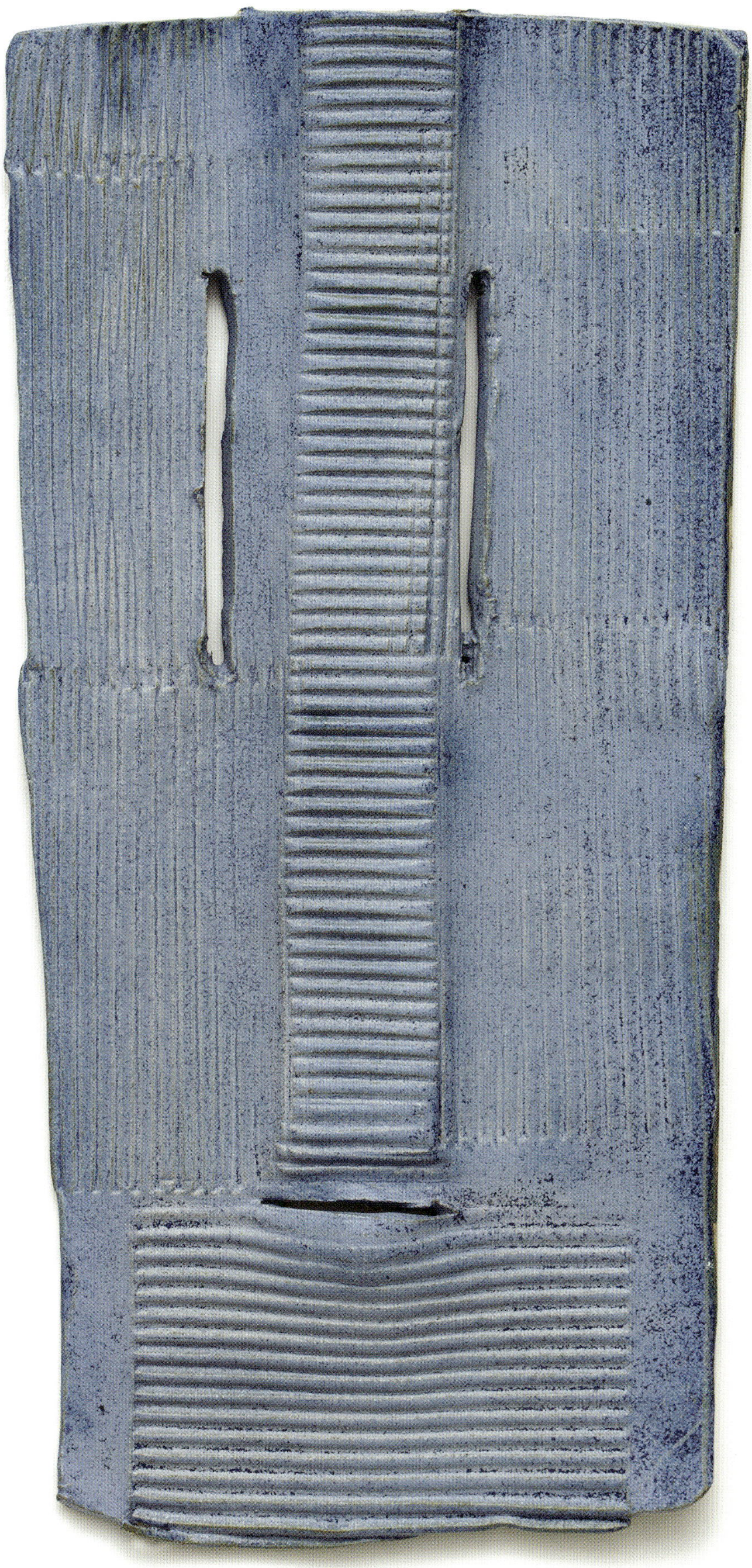

Be-Motz, 2019

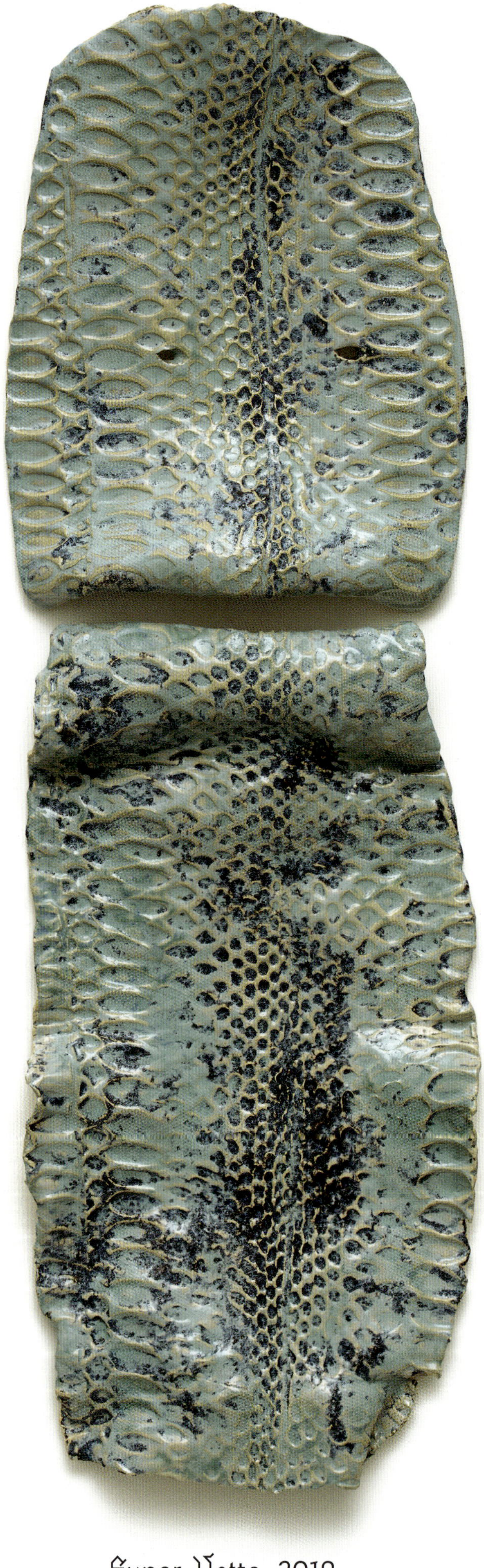

Super-Vette, 2019

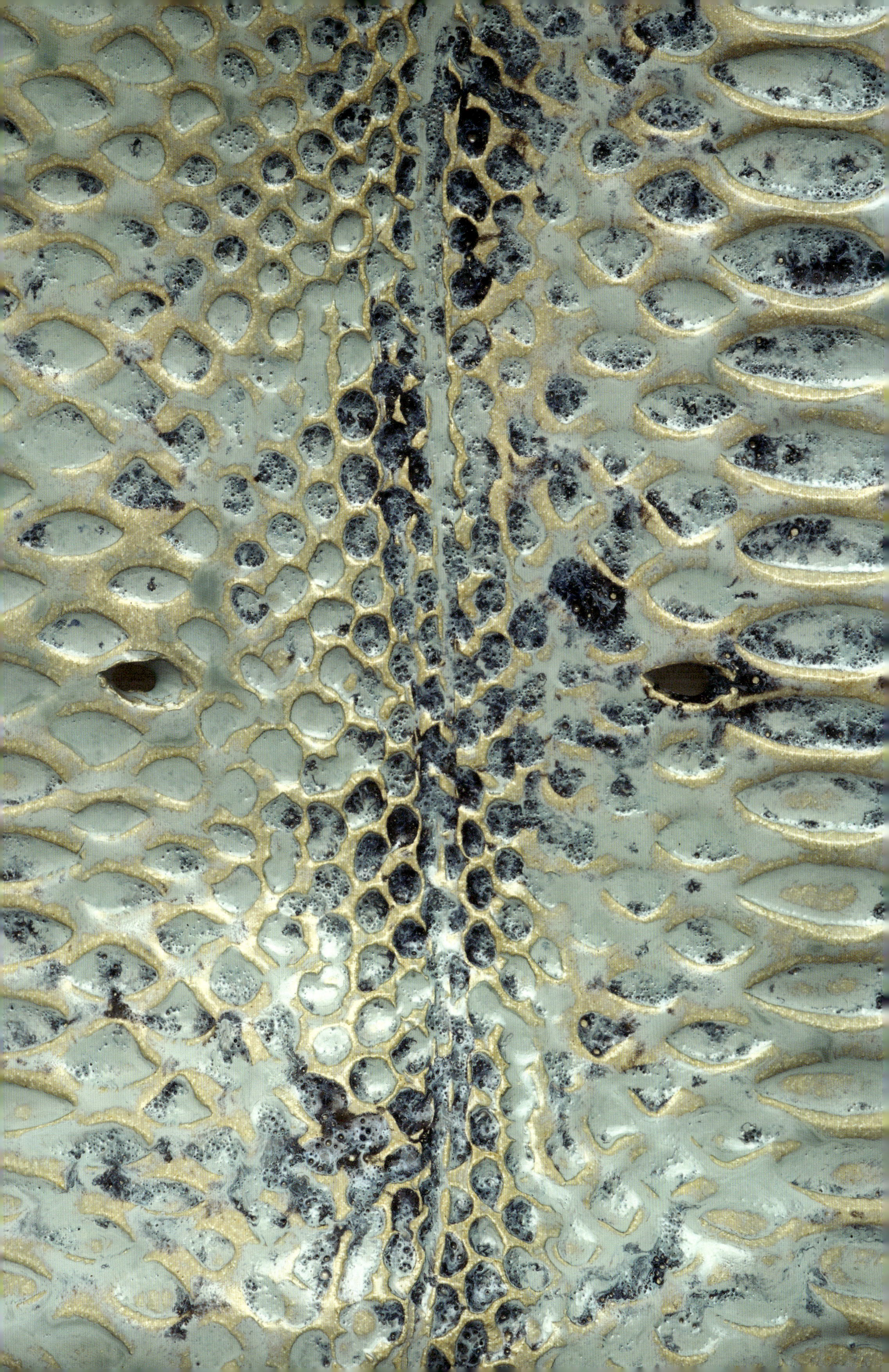

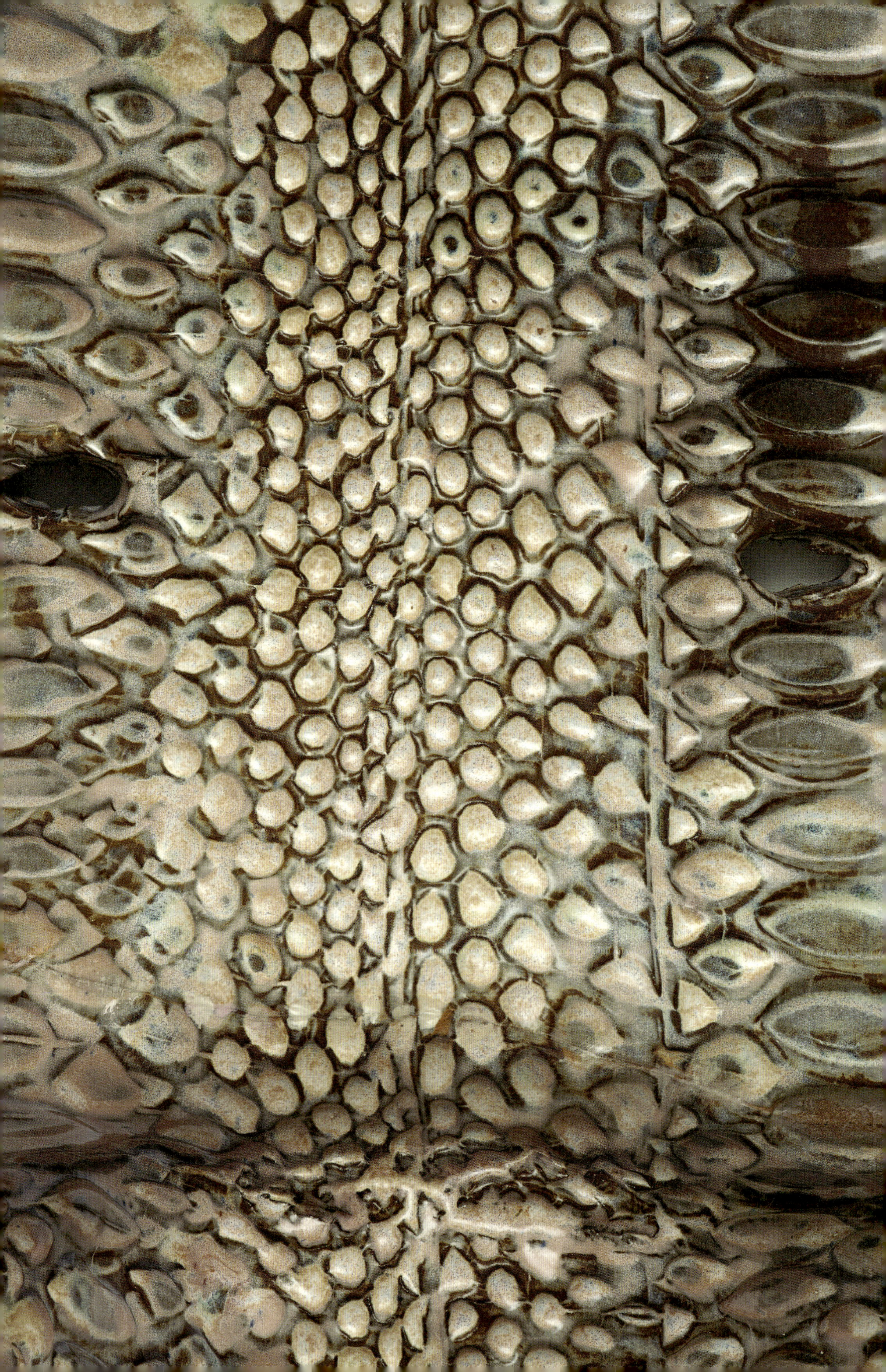

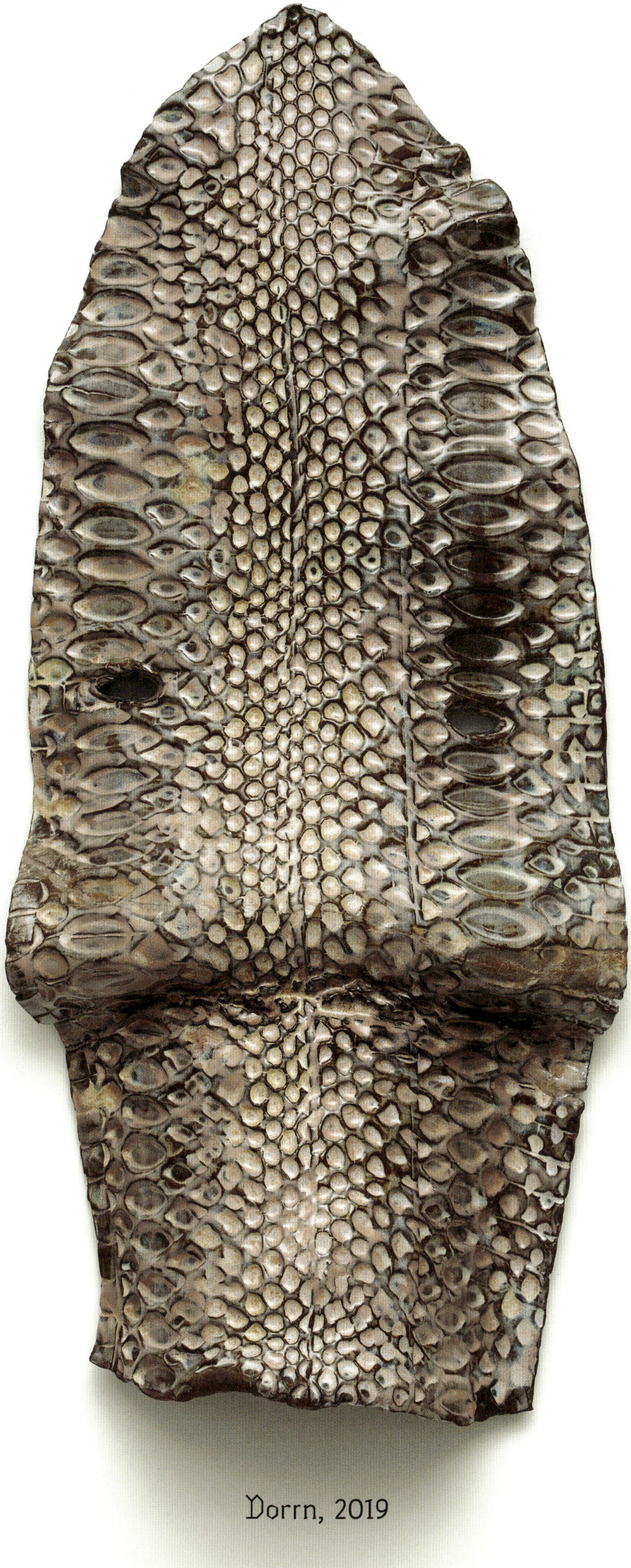

Dorrn, 2019

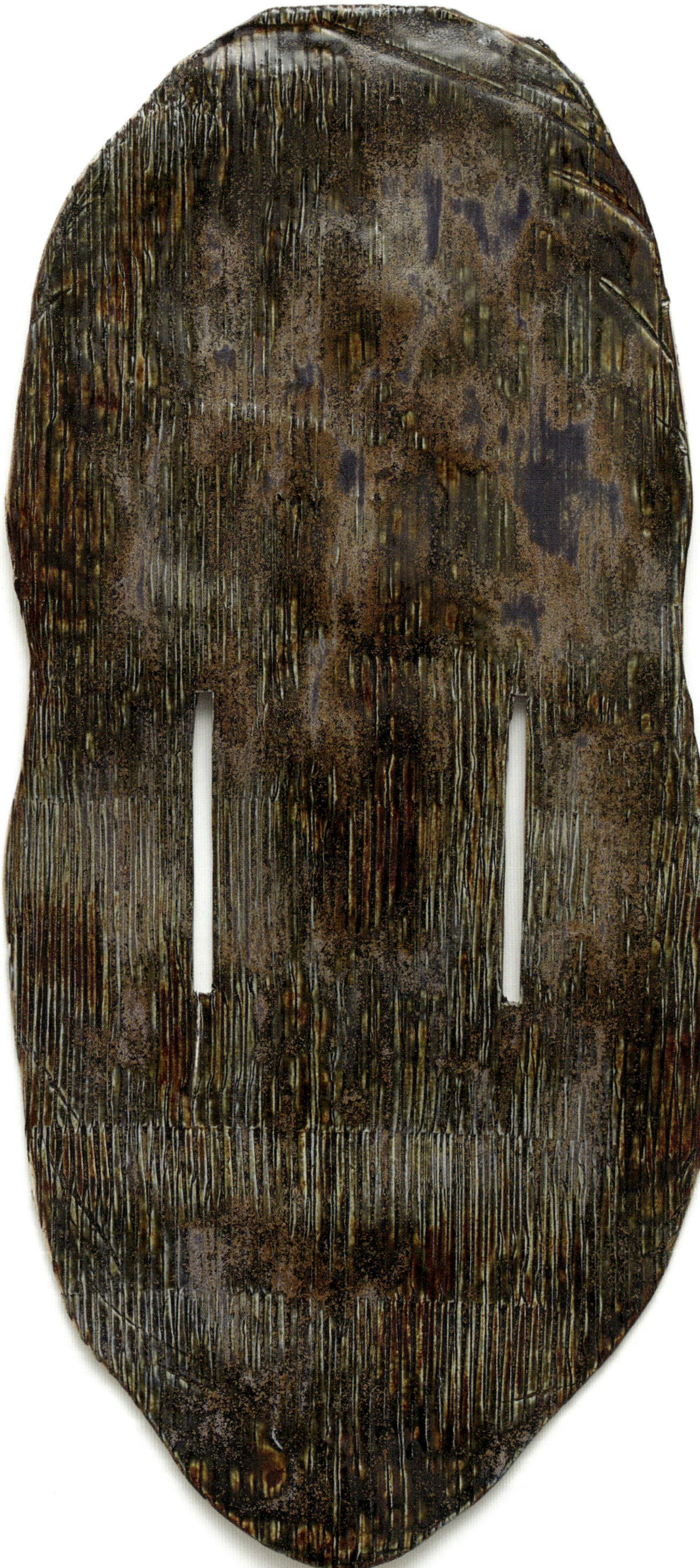

Akin, 2019

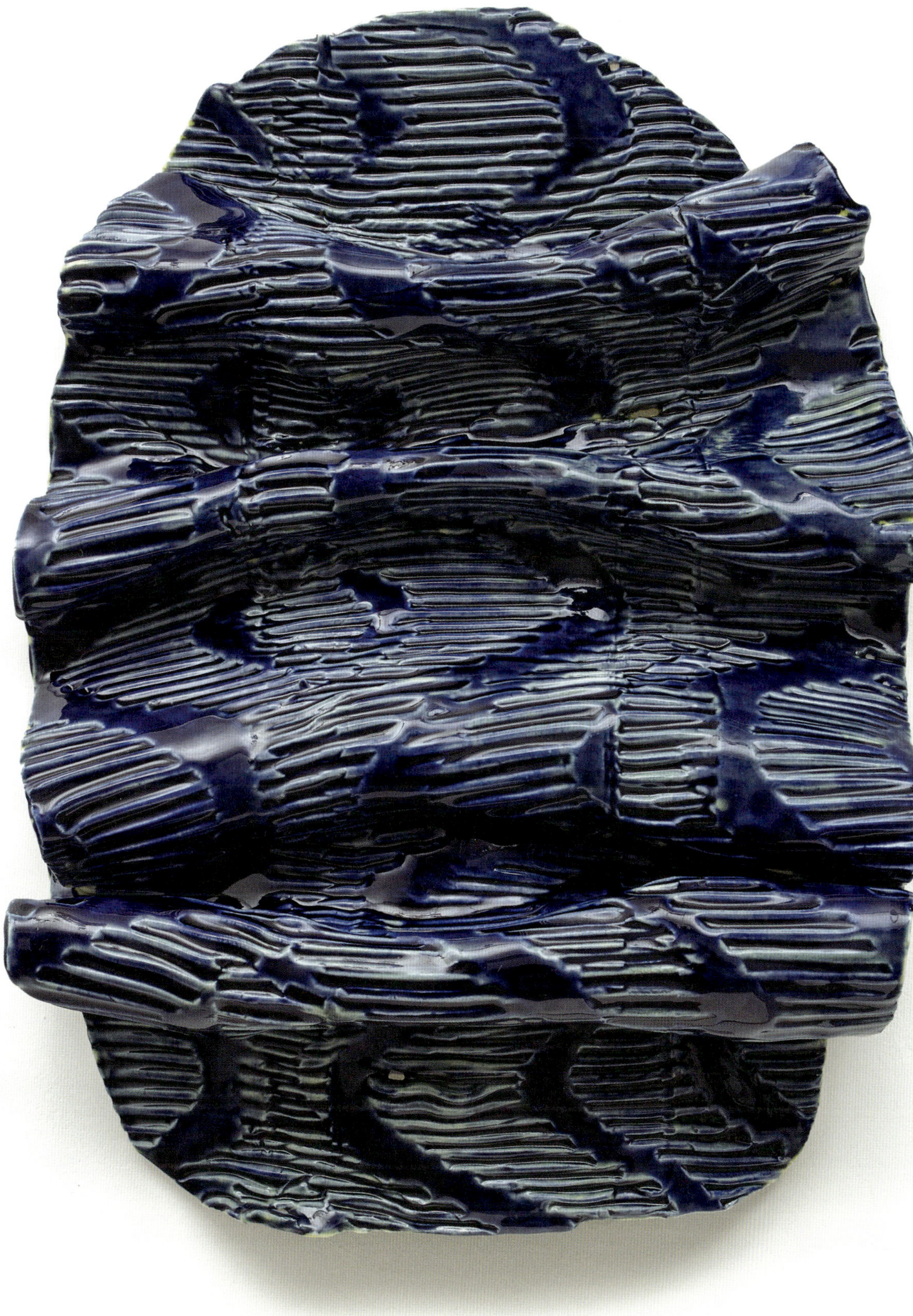

Chris Y., 2019

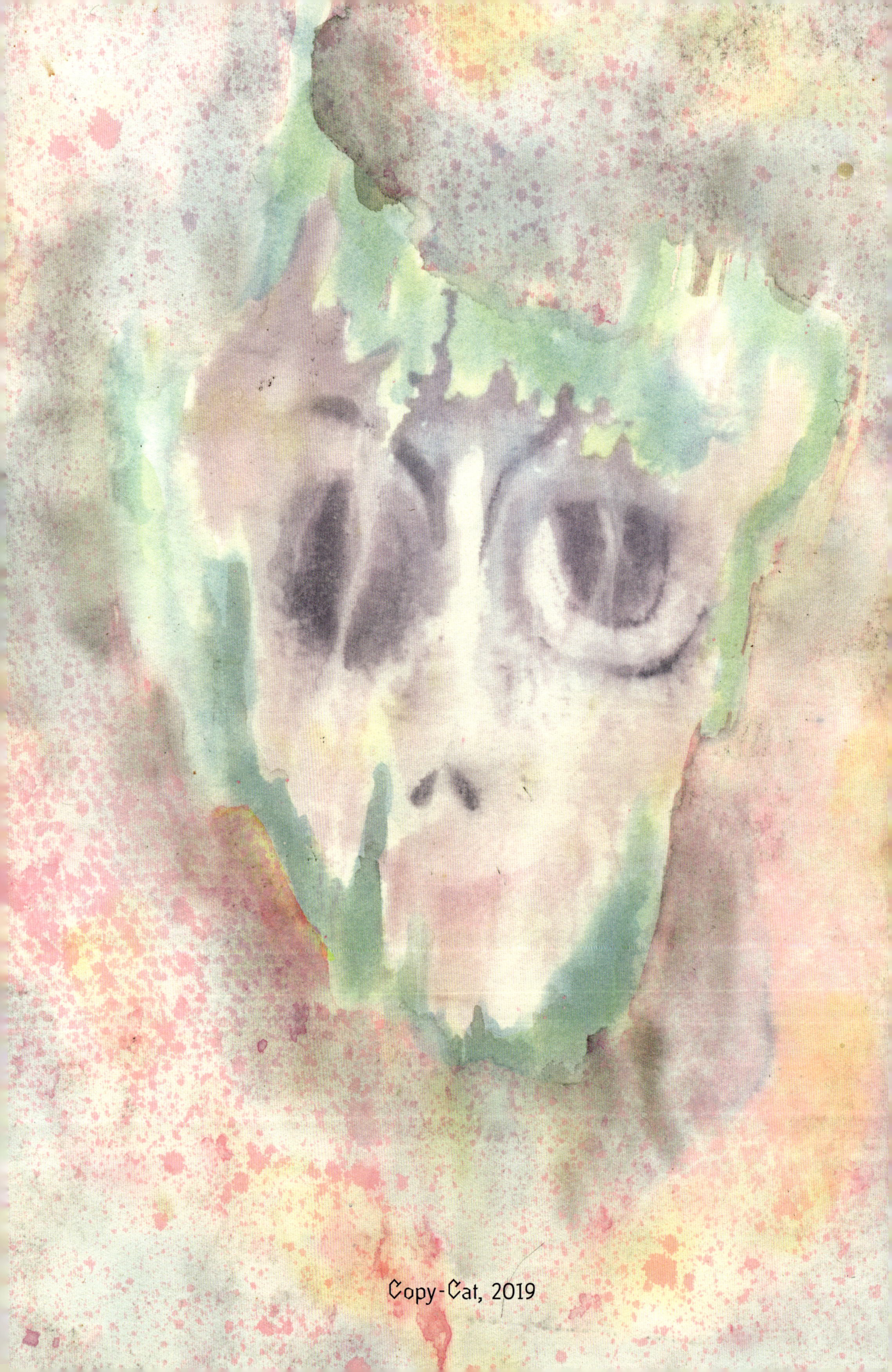

Copy-Cat, 2019

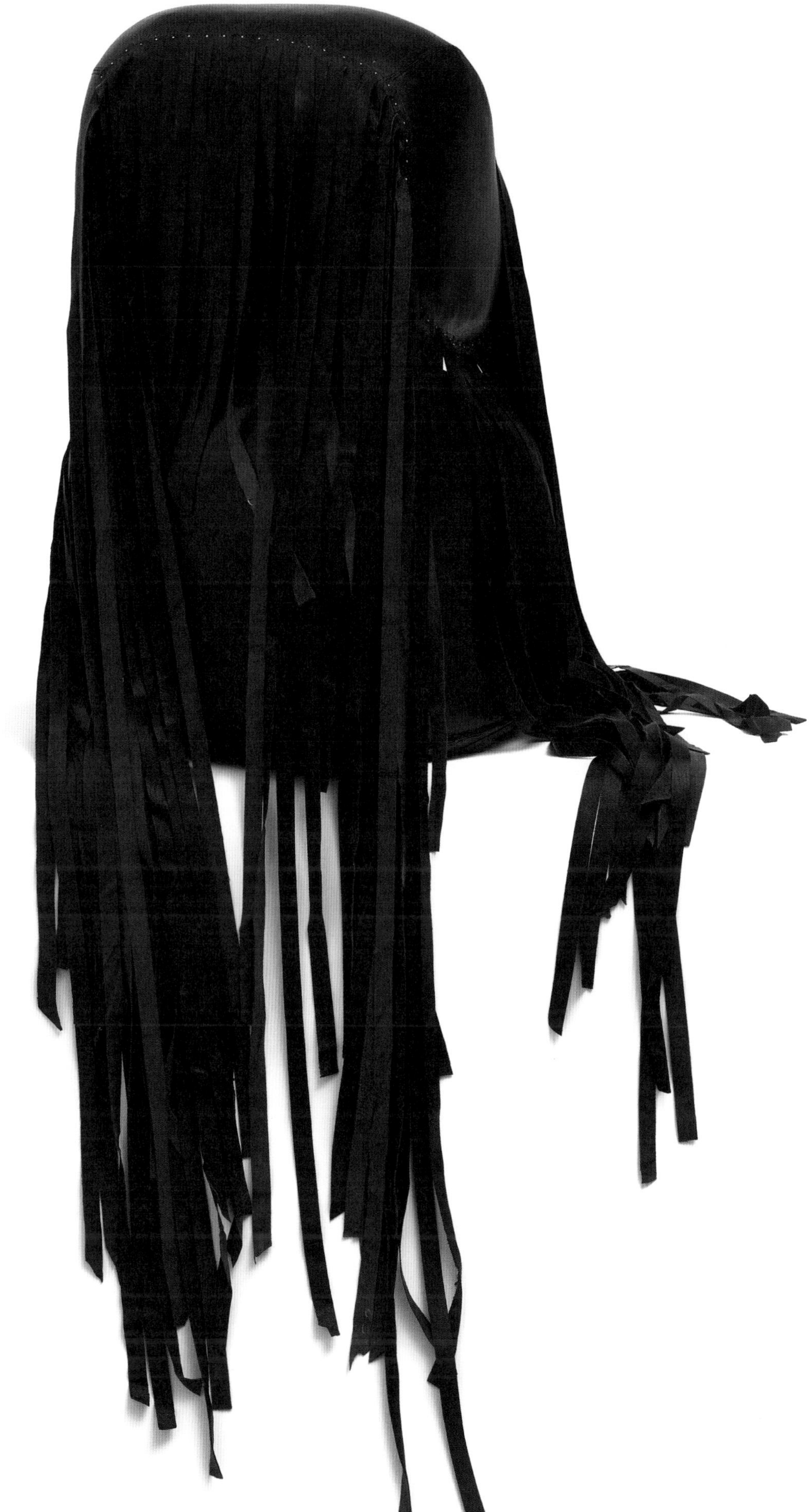

Meute 11, 2019

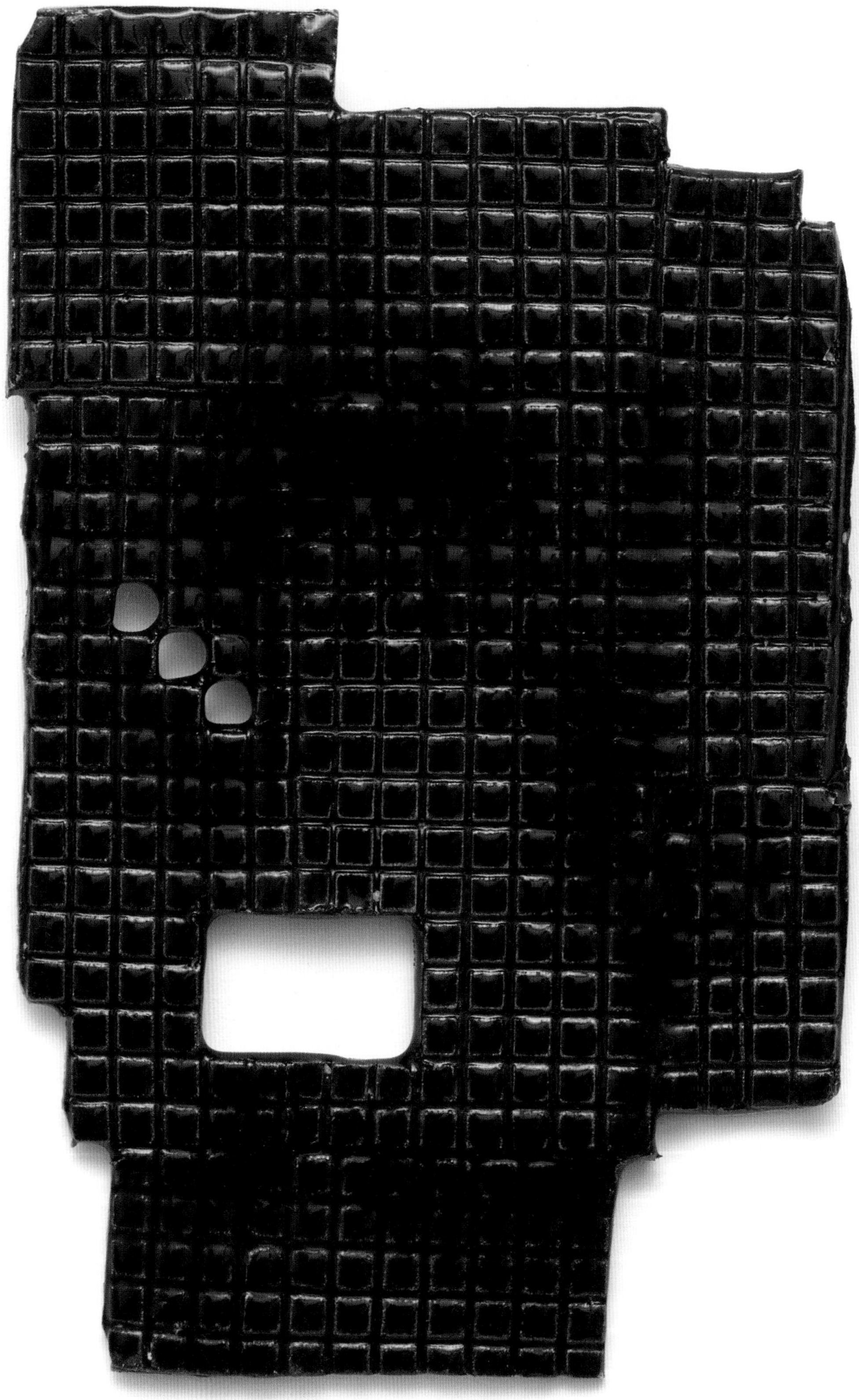

Martha, 2019

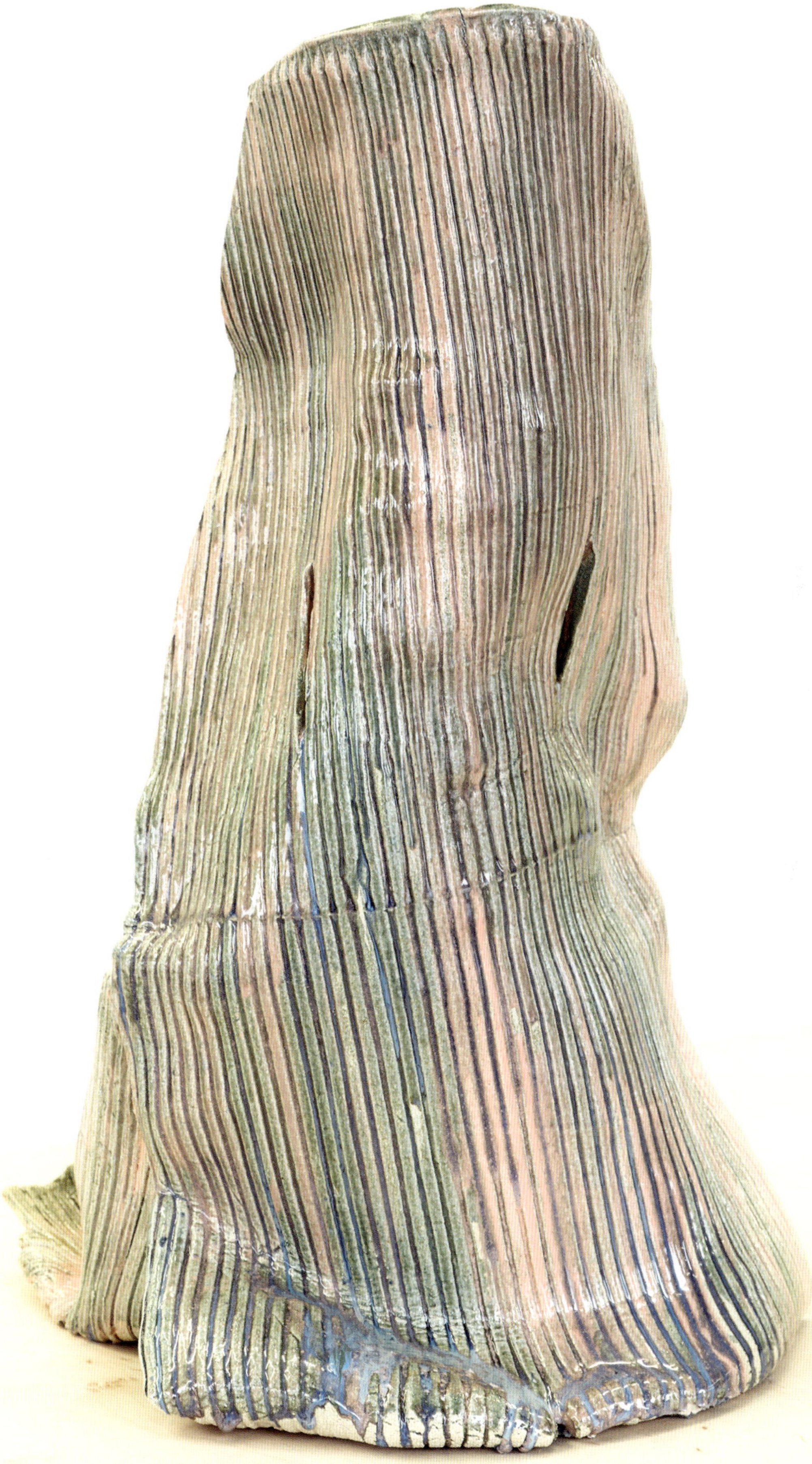

Trunkk P., 2018

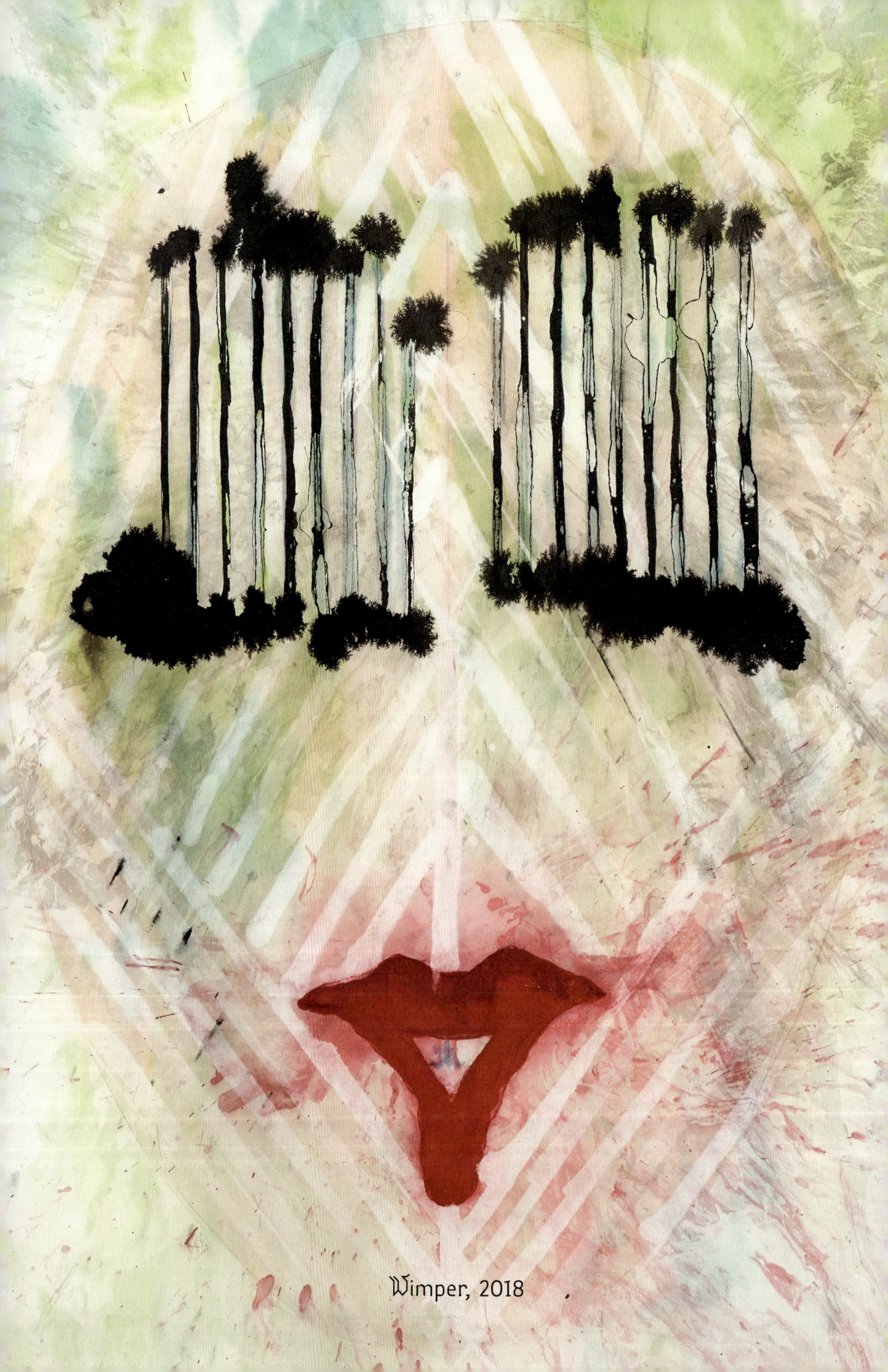

Wimper, 2018

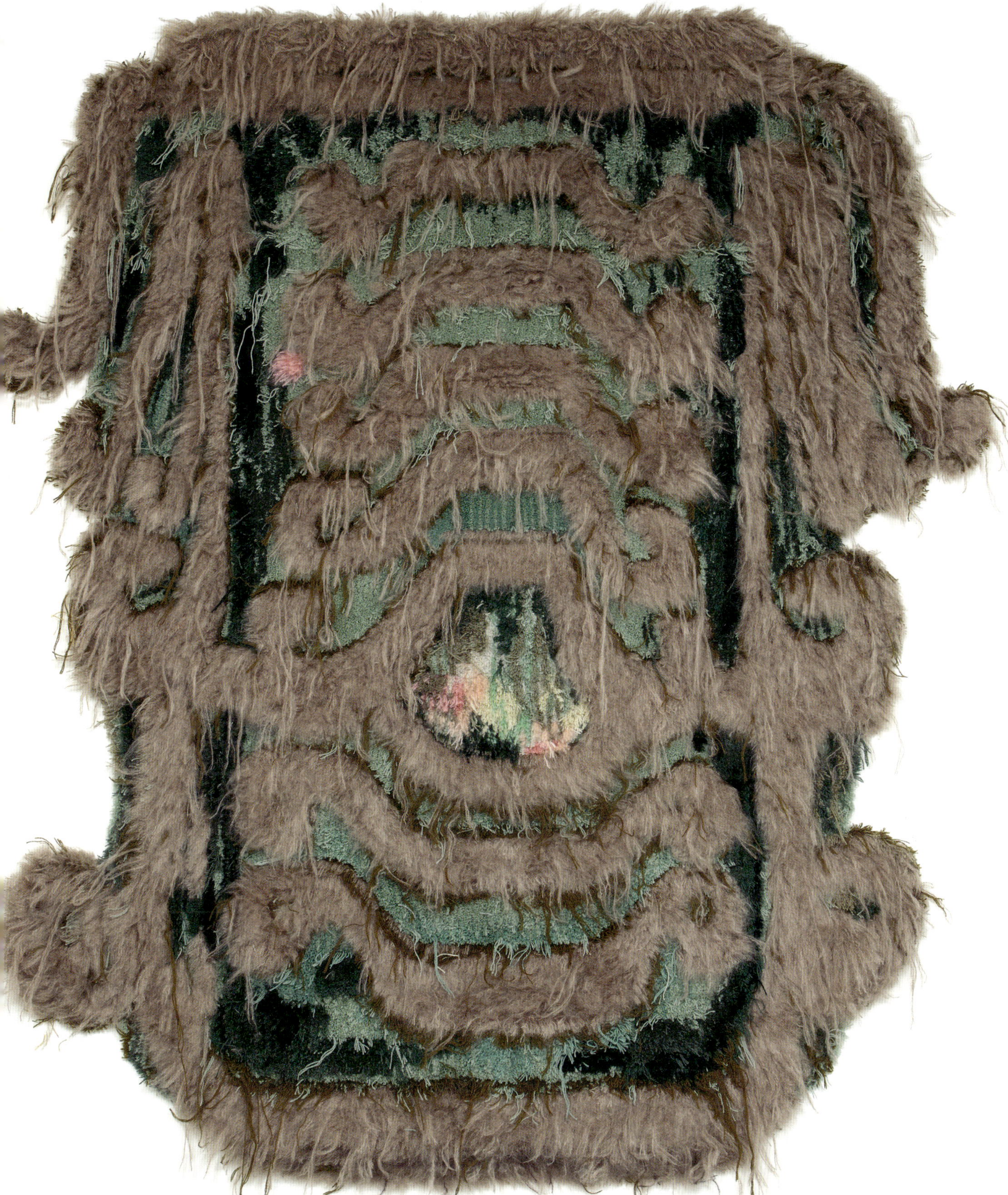

Mart'an G'rl, 2019

Caroline Achaintre & Oriane Durand

Between the Domestic and the Uncanny
The Guiding Thread

Oriane Durand (OD): You did an apprenticeship as a blacksmith, then studied art in Halle and later in London at Chelsea College and Goldsmiths College. How did you get involved in art?

Caroline Achaintre (CA): Of course, I already had an affinity for art in my school days, but ultimately it happened through making. I've always done a lot of drawing, that was one thing. But actually, it came from doing crafts – because of the tactile quality. I definitely did not want to go straight from school into the next institution. I wanted to experience life, so first I did some traveling. Then I decided to do an apprenticeship in a craft and was drawn more and more to art. In Halle, it was a bit of both. You could study metal sculpture there, and as a blacksmith, that made sense to me. But studying metal sculpture was also problematic for me because it was too narrowly focused on the material aspects. From that point on, I wanted to discard that whole material element. So I went away again and looked for something more abstract. When I arrived in London, something very exciting was happening with the Young British Artists movement. A new conceptualism where thematic ideas and materiality went hand in hand and reinforced one another, often with humorous results. This combination of an original idea and a process, which provides a framework but also leaves you plenty of leeway, working spontaneously, taking the associations that accumulate as you are working and pushing them forward, that was the way for me.

OD: How did you go from metal (a hard material) to wool (a soft material)?

Caroline Achaintre & Oriane Durand

Zwischen dem Heimlichen und dem Unheimlichen: der leitende Faden

Oriane Durand (OD): Du hast zuerst eine Ausbildung zur Schmiedin gemacht, dann Kunst in Halle und später in London am Chelsea College und am Goldsmiths College studiert. Wie bist du zur Kunst gekommen?

Caroline Achaintre (CA): Ich hatte natürlich als Schülerin schon eine Affinität zur Kunst, aber letztendlich ging es über das Machen. Ich habe immer viel gezeichnet, das war die eine Sache. Aber eigentlich lief es über das Basteln – wegen der haptischen Qualität. Ich wollte auf keinen Fall direkt von der Schule in die nächste Institution. Ich wollte das Leben spüren und ging erst mal auf Reisen. Dann entschied ich mich für eine handwerkliche Ausbildung und wurde immer mehr von der Kunst angezogen. In Halle war es etwas von beidem. Man konnte dort Metallbildhauerei studieren, und als Schmiedin war das sinnvoll. Aber das Studium war für mich auch problematisch, weil es doch sehr auf das Material reduziert war. Ab dem Punkt wollte ich diese ganze Materialität abwerfen. Deshalb ging ich auch wieder weg, ich suchte nach etwas Abstrakterem. Als ich nach London kam, fand dort mit den Young British Artists gerade etwas sehr Spannendes statt. Ein neuer Konzeptualismus, in dem sich Materialität und Thematik Hand in Hand gegenseitig bestärkten und dadurch auch manchmal Humor hatten. Diese Mischung aus einer Ursprungsidee und einem Prozess, der einen Rahmen gibt und zugleich viel Spielraum lässt, spontan zu arbeiten, sprich dabei die eigenen Assoziationen, die sich während des Arbeitens aufbauen, weiter zu pushen, das war für mich der Weg.

OD: Wie bist du vom Metall – einem harten Material – zur Wolle – einem weichen Material – gekommen?

CA: I don't distinguish between them that much. Metal never really interested me as an art material and I never really had anything to do with wool, either. It was more a matter of my need to find an intensity in my work. At Goldsmiths, I started making lots of small ink drawings. Shortly before that, I was still working on a larger scale. I absolutely wanted to achieve the intensity of these small drawings in larger, more spacious objects. These drawings already had to do with masks and portraits, but also with the uncanny — in Freud's sense. Uncanny actually means something familiar that makes your flesh creep when it's in a unfamiliar context. It comes across, for example, in the story "The Sandman," by E. T. A. Hoffmann: you suddenly see something that's already familiar in a different light. I thought, if I'm already working with the uncanny, a term which in German (*unheimlich*) contains the word for "home," it would be interesting to choose a material that comes from a domestic (*Heim*) context. That's how I arrived at wool.

OD: Where did things go from there?

CA: I had these drawings that I thought I would like to make into a domestic object. Then a rug was the obvious idea because it comes from the home, after all. Later, I had to decide whether the rug should be displayed on the floor or the wall. In order to avoid the constant question of whether people would be allowed to walk on it, and because of the way perspective gets distorted when a portrait is on the floor, I quickly decided to make it a wall hanging. Almost a tapestry, something you can hang on the wall like a picture. Of course I didn't know how to produce a rug. I went to a textile workshop, where they showed me a tufting gun — it looks a little like a power drill and makes it possible to mechanize the knotting process. I simply tried to recreate a drawing using the tufting technique. The first attempt was black and white and much more organized, but it already had this relief character. Because an image results from individual pixels or woolen threads, the work immediately took on a certain intensity, like the drawings but different.

OD: The process of tufting also has an intensively physical, highly performative quality. You stretch a piece of canvas, hold

CA: Ich mache da gar nicht so viel Unterschied. Das Metall hat mich als Kunstmaterial nie wirklich interessiert, auch mit Wolle habe ich nie etwas zu tun gehabt. Es kam eher aus meinem Bedürfnis, in den Arbeiten eine Intensität zu finden. Am Goldsmiths habe ich angefangen, ziemlich viele kleine Tintenzeichnungen anzufertigen. Kurz davor hatte ich noch große Objekte hergestellt. Ich wollte unbedingt die Intensität dieser kleinen Zeichnungen im Großen und im Räumlichen erreichen. Diese Zeichnungen hatten schon mit der Maske und den Porträts zu tun, aber eben auch mit dem Unheimlichen – im Sinn von Freud, vom englischen *uncanny*. *Uncanny* ist eigentlich etwas Vertrautes, in einem anderen Kontext ist es aber etwas, das einem unter die Haut geht. Wie es beispielsweise bei E. T. A. Hoffmann in der Geschichte vom *Sandmann* zu lesen ist: Etwas, das man schon kennt, sieht man plötzlich in einem anderen Licht. Ich dachte, wenn ich schon mit dem Unheimlichen arbeite, in dem das Heimliche, auch das Heim drinsteckt, dann wäre es interessant, ein Material auszuwählen, das aus einem heimischen Kontext stammt. So bin ich zur Wolle gekommen.

OD: Wie ging es dann weiter?

CA: Ich hatte diese Zeichnungen und dachte, ich würde gerne ein *domestic object* daraus machen. Die Idee zum Teppich kam dann wie von selbst, weil er ja aus dem Heim kommt. Später musste ich mich entscheiden, ob der Teppich auf den Boden oder an der Wand gezeigt wird. Um die ständige Frage, ob es erlaubt sei, darauf rumzulaufen, zu vermeiden und aufgrund der perspektivischen Verzerrung eines „Porträts" am Boden habe ich mich dann doch sehr schnell für die Wand entschieden. Quasi für eine Tapisserie, etwas, das man wie ein Bild an die Wand hängen kann. Ich wusste natürlich nicht, wie man einen Teppich herstellt. Ich ging in eine Textilwerkstatt, in der mir eine Tuftpistole gezeigt wurde – sie sieht ein bisschen aus wie eine Bohrmaschine und ermöglicht eine Mechanisierung des Vorgangs des Knüpfens. Ich probierte einfach, mit der Technik des Tuftens eine Zeichnung umzusetzen. Der erste Versuch war nur schwarz-weiß und viel geordneter, hatte aber schon diesen Reliefcharakter. Weil ein Bild aus einzelnen Pixeln bzw. Wollfäden

this gun-like electrical machine, which is attached to an air compressor, in your hand and shoot wool from behind through the canvas. You don't see the result right away; you always have to work back to front.

CA: Yes, it's really a very physical process. And I need that. Making your body a part of your work is an aspect that is important for me in any case. For example, I wouldn't be able to weave; that would be too restricted and slow for me. And as far as shape is concerned, you can work very freely with the tufting technique.

OD: Your language of form or iconography is rich and diverse. For me, every new rug is a surprise; it creates a kind of compulsion to see the next one. But there are two aspects that always recur in wall tapestries and ceramics: the archaic, or an aesthetic that reminds you of what we call naïve art, and, as you've already mentioned, the uncanny.

CA: I like to take inspiration from ethnological collections, the first objects made by humans, from prehistoric sculptures and images to album covers by heavy metal bands. The uncanny comes from the selection of motifs. They are mostly characters, portraits, faces, or masks, with the masks increasingly becoming characters. Very often, two creatures coexist in one work. I look for a kind of conflict through a coexistence of multipersonality; it doesn't have to have anything to do with schizophrenia, it can also be in the shamanic sense. I also think that we have more than one person in ourselves. Sometimes it remains unclear what someone sees or perceives in my works. But the uncanny is also expressed in the use of a broad palette of colors, in the warmth and softness of the wool itself, and in its attractiveness. There is a duality between rational and irrational; these ideas actually aren't opposed to each other.

OD: What kind of relationship do you have to the portraits and faces? In reference to Freud, do you understand them as likenesses or reflections of yourself?

entsteht, bekam die Arbeit sofort eine gewisse Intensität, wie die Zeichnungen, nur anders.

OD: Der Prozess des Tuftens hat auch etwas intensiv Körperliches, etwas stark Performatives. Du spannst ein Stück Leinwand, hältst diese pistolenähnliche elektrische Maschine, die an einen Luftkompressor angeschlossen ist, in der Hand und schießt Wolle von hinten durch die Leinwand. Man sieht das Ergebnis nicht sofort, sondern muss immer von hinten nach vorn gehen.

CA: Ja, es ist wirklich ein sehr physischer Prozess. Und ich brauche das. Der körperliche Einsatz in der Arbeit ist auf jeden Fall ein Aspekt, der für mich wichtig ist. Ich könnte zum Beispiel nicht weben; das wäre mir zu langwierig und zu klein. Und was die Form angeht, kann man mit der Technik des Tufting ganz frei arbeiten.

OD: Deine Formensprache beziehungsweise Ikonografie ist reich und divers. Für mich ist jeder neue Teppich eine Überraschung; es entsteht quasi eine Sucht, den nächsten sehen zu wollen. Dennoch gibt es zwei Aspekte, die in den Wandteppichen und auch in der Keramik immer wiederkehren: das Archaische beziehungsweise eine Ästhetik, die an das, was man „naive Kunst" nennt, erinnert, und, wie du vorhin schon erwähnt hast, das Unheimliche.

CA: Ich lasse mich gern von ethnologischen Sammlungen, den ersten Objekten der Menschheit, von prähistorischen Skulpturen und Abbildungen bis hin zu Plattencovern von Heavy-Metal-Bands inspirieren. Das Unheimliche kommt von der Auswahl der Motive. Es sind meistens Charaktere, Porträts, Gesichter oder Masken, wobei die Masken immer mehr zu Charakteren geworden sind. Sehr oft findet sich eine Koexistenz von zwei Kreaturen in einer Arbeit. Ich suche über eine Koexistenz von *multipersonality* eine Art Konflikt; das muss aber nichts mit Schizophrenie zu tun haben, es kann auch im schamanischen Sinne sein. Auch denke ich, dass wir mehr als eine Person in uns haben. Manchmal bleibt es unklar, was man in meinen Arbeiten sieht oder wahrnimmt.

CA: Not consciously, but certainly unconsciously. For me, it's often about dialogue. You find the works, but they also find you, so that sometimes the result is something different from what you expected. As in Frankenstein's lab, they are my creatures. The abstract works are still creatures, at least the skins of creatures. Somehow they seem to me to be objects with souls. Without this dialogue, I think I would find it hard to create something.

OD: It also goes beyond that. The bridge from object to subject belongs to the realm of animism.

CA: Wool is a dead material, but it does come from the organic world. With clay, I try to breathe a certain life into the material. I purposely sought out an extreme material, one that is not neutral at all. Hair and wool are warm, but they're also a little bit disgusting. Clay is also alive. I think the division is not really that stark; there are always ambiguities. That's why my work is not highly verbal, I think there's more to it than mentioning facts.

OD: From animism you arrive at the aspect of the fetish. Fetishism in the religious sense means the belief in supernatural, personal, or impersonal powers, which inhabit certain objects and are honored as holy things. Do you see forms of fetishism in your work or does the concept have any importance for you?

CA: First of all, I find both meanings of the word *fetish* very interesting: the fetish that is celebrated in other cultures, as well as fetish in a sexual context. In both cases, extraordinary power or meaning is attributed to an object, loaded onto it so to speak. It's irrational, and I find that exciting. Wool and leather, both materials that I like to use, have a very strong aura. One of them emits warmth and can be compared with hair, fur, or feathers. The other one emits power, strength, and potency and is actually a skin.

OD: In your personal development, you went from wall hanging to ceramics. How did that happen?

Das Unheimliche drückt sich aber auch in der Anwendung einer breit gefächerten Farbenpalette, in der Wärme und der Weichheit der Wolle an sich, auch in ihrer Attraktivität aus. Es gibt darin eine Zweischneidigkeit zwischen rational und irrational; diese Vorstellungen stehen eigentlich gar nicht so sehr im Gegensatz zueinander.

OD: Wie ist dein Verhältnis zu den Porträts und Gesichtern? In Referenz zu Freud: Verstehst du sie als Eben- oder Spiegelbilder von dir?

CA: Nicht bewusst, ganz sicher aber unbewusst. Mir geht es oft um den Dialog. Man findet die Arbeiten, und sie finden einen aber auch, sodass manchmal etwas anderes herauskommt, als man sich im Vorhinein vorgestellt hat. Wie bei Frankenstein sind sie Kreaturen von mir. Die abstrakten Arbeiten sind immer noch Kreaturen, zumindest die Häute von Kreaturen. Irgendwie sind sie für mich Objekte mit Seele. Ohne diesen Dialog, denke ich, fände ich es schwierig, etwas zu kreieren.

OD: Es geht also darüber hinaus. Der Übergang vom Objekt zum Subjekt fällt in den Bereich des Animismus.

CA: Die Wolle ist zwar ein totes Material, kommt aber aus dem Organischen. Beim Ton versuche ich, dem Material wieder ein gewisses Leben einzuhauchen. Ich habe mir bewusst ein extremes Material ausgesucht, eines, das überhaupt nicht neutral ist. Haare und Wolle sind ja schon warm, aber auch ein bisschen eklig. Ton ist auch lebendig. Ich glaube, dass die Trennung nicht so stark ist; es gibt immer Zwischendeutungen. Deshalb arbeite ich nicht so stark verbal, ich glaube, es gibt etwas anderes als Fakten, die genannt werden.

OD: Vom Animismus gelangt man zum Aspekt des Fetischs. Fetischismus bezeichnet im religiösen Sinn den Glauben an übernatürliche, persönliche oder unpersönliche Mächte, die in bestimmten Gegenständen wohnen und als heilige Objekte verehrt werden. Siehst du in deinen Arbeiten Formen von Fetischismus beziehungsweise spielt das Konzept überhaupt eine Rolle für dich?

CA: I always wanted to be a sculptor, but I can't seem to get away from the wall. That's where it starts. With these rugs, which are like reliefs, there is an object quality, but ultimately they work like painting. Like my ink drawings, they are extensions of painting. With old drawings, I've also tried to make masks out of paper. Paper has something spontaneous, you can glue it together or staple it quickly. I like to create objects from flat material. That way you can see really clearly how the three-dimensional forms are created. But I don't think paper has any lifespan as a sculptural material. I used paper that was too flimsy, too thin. Then I thought, I'll try it with ceramic and do a version of what I had already done with paper. I wanted the result to be thin and delicate, or the process – the folding and "gluing together" of the clay slabs – to lead from a flat material to a three-dimensional one and for the hollow part of the work to be visible. I didn't want to reinforce anything, I didn't want it to become thick or for the handwork to be hidden. A clay work is often glazed over in such a way that the process is no longer evident.

OD: How do you conceive of your exhibition? How do you proceed with it?

CA: There's a common thread running through the work. I don't completely redefine myself for every exhibition. There are always aspects that emerge more strongly. For the exhibition *Dissolver* in Dortmund, I wanted to get into the psychedelic realm. During that time, I wanted to work with an optical sensory overload. In the end, it actually developed into things that emerge and then optically dissolve. The word *dissolver* makes you think of chemistry, which is an aspect of the psychedelic, and it also refers to images that either dissolve or transform when you look at them. In the work *Bat-8*, which I made for the exhibition, I see a bat and an octopus at the same time, and of course there's a skull in there as well. On the other hand, the dissolution in the work *Neptun*, which "only" shows the face of a bearded male figure, comes from the intensive mixing and melding of threads of various colors and lengths.

OD: For your wall tapestries and ceramics, you're not just concerned with achieving technical perfection, but with exploring

CA: Zuallererst finde ich beide Bedeutungen des Wortes Fetisch sehr interessant: sowohl den Fetisch, der in anderen Kulturen zelebriert wird, als auch den Fetisch im sexuellen Kontext. In beiden Fällen wird einem Objekt außerordentliche Kraft oder Bedeutung beigemessen, sozusagen aufgeladen. Das ist irrational, und das finde ich spannend. Wolle und Leder, beides Materialien, die ich gerne benutze, haben eine starke Ausstrahlung. Das eine strahlt Wärme aus und kann mit Haar, Fell oder Federn verglichen werden. Das andere strahlt Kraft, Stärke und Potenz aus und ist eben eine Haut.

OD: In deiner persönlichen Entwicklung bist du von den Wandteppichen zu den Keramiken gekommen. Was ist passiert?

CA: Ich wollte immer Bildhauerin sein, komme aber quasi nie von der Wand weg. Da fängt es schon mal an. Mit diesen Teppichen, die wie Reliefs sind, gibt es zwar eine Objekthaftigkeit, aber letztendlich funktionieren sie wie Malerei. Sie sind, wie meine Tintenzeichnungen, Verlängerungen der Malerei. Mit alten Zeichnungen habe ich aber auch versucht, Masken aus Papier zu machen. Papier hat etwas Spontanes, kann schnell zusammengeklebt oder getackert werden. Ich mag es, Objekte aus einem flächigen Material zu schaffen. Man kann dabei gut nachvollziehen, wie es zu diesen dreidimensionalen Formen kommt. Aber Papier hat für mich keine Dauerhaftigkeit als skulpturales Material. Ich verwendete Papier, das, wie man im Englischen sagt, *flimsy* war, zu nachgiebig, zu dünn. Dann dachte ich, ich versuche es mal mit Keramik, und setzte das um, was ich schon mit Papier gemacht hatte. Ich wollte, dass das Ergebnis dünn und filigran wird beziehungsweise dass der Prozess – das Falten und „Zusammenkleben" der Tonplatten – vom flachen Material zu einer dreidimensionalen Form führt, das Hohle in der Arbeit sichtbar wird. Ich wollte nichts aufbauen, ich wollte nicht, dass es dick wird, dass die Handarbeit versteckt wird. Oft wird eine Tonarbeit zugeschmiert, sodass der Prozess nicht mehr nachvollziehbar ist.

OD: Wie konzipierst du deine Ausstellungen? Wie gehst du dabei vor?

the tension between the representational and the abstract. Many of your works, such as *Bat-8*, but also ceramics such as *Monmec*, represent hybrid characters. They are reminiscent of Surrealist creatures like those of Max Ernst, but also of picture puzzles and Rorschach tests. Do you also feel a particular affinity for Surrealism?

CA: Definitely! In Surrealism, there are also a lot of doublings or forms that change the meaning of materials, as with Meret Oppenheim's fur-lined cup. Elsa Schiaparelli's dresses also play with that, Salvador Dalí's lobster telephone, Hans Bellmer's dolls. And importantly, there is a lot of humor. A sense of humor that you don't have to explain, or that can't even be explained.

OD: How do you decide on a title? For example, why is one work called *Neptun*?

CA: I work with the titles in a way that's fairly associative. They often come later. *Neptun* is the god of the sea in Roman mythology. Here he seems to have just emerged from the sea; blue and green "paint" is still dripping from him. The gray and green threads could also be hairs, beard hairs, or algae: it has to do with the mood created by the shape and colors. Once the work is born, it is named for what I see in it. It doesn't always have to be what I planned.

OD: What are you planning for your exhibition at the Belvedere?

CA: It's only now gradually taking shape. My first interest was in the cockroach's shell and the question of how creatures like cockroaches fit into dystopian worlds. I'm fascinated by films like Neill Blomkamp's *District 9* (2009), and I've also been thinking about the story of Gregor Samsa in Franz Kafka's *The Metamorphosis* (1912) again, but I do notice that I'm already getting away from that, and the exhibition might become a dream version of the animal world. At any rate, the exhibition architecture I am planning for the Belvedere 21 interferes with the existing space, and, again, I work with what I find. The ceiling is rather low there, I imagine it as something

CA: Die Arbeit durchzieht ein roter Faden. Ich definiere mich nicht für jede Ausstellung komplett neu. Es gibt immer Aspekte, die stärker herauskommen. Für die Ausstellung *DISSOLVER* in Dortmund wollte ich ins Psychedelische gehen. Ich wollte in jener Zeit mit einer optischen Reizüberflutung arbeiten. Am Ende hat es sich eher hin zu Dingen, die entstehen und sich optisch gleich wieder auflösen, entwickelt. Das Wort *dissolver* – auf Deutsch Lösungsmittel – vermittelt einerseits die Idee der Chemie, die im Psychedelischen vorhanden ist, und weist andererseits auf Bilder hin, die sich beim Betrachten entweder auflösen oder verwandeln. In der Arbeit *Bat-8*, die ich für die Ausstellung gemacht habe, stecken für mich zugleich eine Fledermaus und ein Oktopus, und natürlich ist auch ein Schädel drin. Die Auflösung in der Arbeit *Neptun*, die „nur" das Gesicht einer bärtigen männlichen Figur zeigt, entsteht dagegen aus der intensiveren Mischung und Verschmelzung unterschiedlich langer verschiedenfarbiger Fäden.

OD: Bei deinen Wandteppichen und Keramiken geht es dir eben nicht darum, technische Perfektion zu erreichen, sondern darum, das Spannungsfeld zwischen dem Figürlichen und dem Abstrakten zu erkunden. Viele deiner Arbeiten, wie *Bat-8*, aber auch Keramiken wie *Monmec* stellen hybride Charaktere dar. Sie erinnern an Kreaturen des Surrealismus wie jene von Max Ernst, aber auch an Vexierbilder und Rorschachtests. Spürst du zum Surrealismus eine besondere Affinität?

CA: Auf jeden Fall! Auch im Surrealismus gibt es oft Doppelungen oder Verschiebungen der Bedeutung der Materialität durch die Form, wie bei Meret Oppenheims Felltasse. Auch Elsa Schiaparellis Kleider spielen damit, Salvador Dalís Hummertelefon, Hans Bellmers Puppen ... Und ganz wichtig, es gibt darin viel Humor. Einen Humor, den man nicht erklären muss beziehungsweise der sich nicht erklären lässt.

OD: Wie kommst du auf die Titel? Warum heißt eine Arbeit zum Beispiel *Neptun*?

CA: Mit den Titeln arbeite ich ziemlich assoziativ. Sie kommen oft später. *Neptun* ist in der römischen Mythologie der Gott des

like a spaceship. A crowded communal area for my creatures, a temporary habitat on the move.

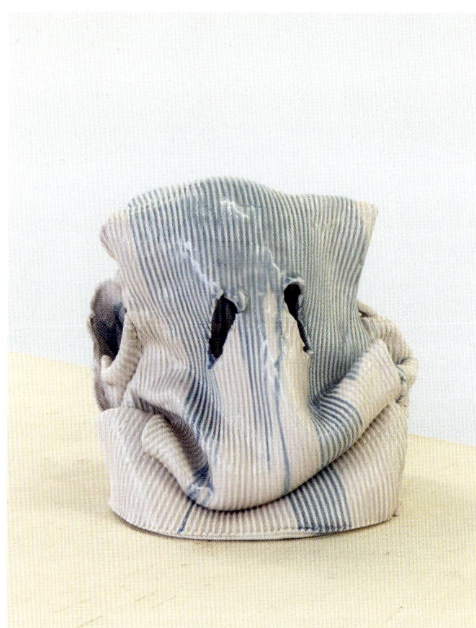

Monmec, 2017

Meeres. Er scheint hier gerade dem Meer entstiegen zu sein, von ihm tropft noch blaue und graue „Farbe". Die grauen und grünen Fäden können sowohl Haare, Barthaare als auch Algen sein: Es hat mit der Stimmung zu tun, die von der Form und den Farben gegeben wird. Wenn die Arbeit geboren ist, wird sie danach benannt, was ich in ihr sehe. Es muss nicht immer das sein, was ich geplant habe.

OD: Was planst du für deine Ausstellung im Belvedere?

CA: Das nimmt erst jetzt so langsam Form an. Mein erstes Interesse galt dem Panzer der Kakerlake und der Frage, wie Kreaturen *wie* eben Kakerlaken in dystopische Welten passen. Filme wie Neill Blomkamps *District 9* (2009) finde ich faszinierend, inzwischen auch wieder die Geschichte von Gregor Samsa in Franz Kafkas *Verwandlung* (1912), aber ich merke schon, wie ich davon abkomme und die Ausstellung vielleicht noch zu einer Traumversion des Animalischen wird. Auf jeden Fall greift die Ausstellungsarchitektur in den bereits vorhandenen Raum ein, und ich arbeite mit Vorgefundenem. Die Decke ist ziemlich niedrig, ich stelle es mir ein bisschen wie in einem Raumschiff vor. Eine gedrängte Sammelkabine für meine Kreaturen, ein temporäres Habitat *on the move.*

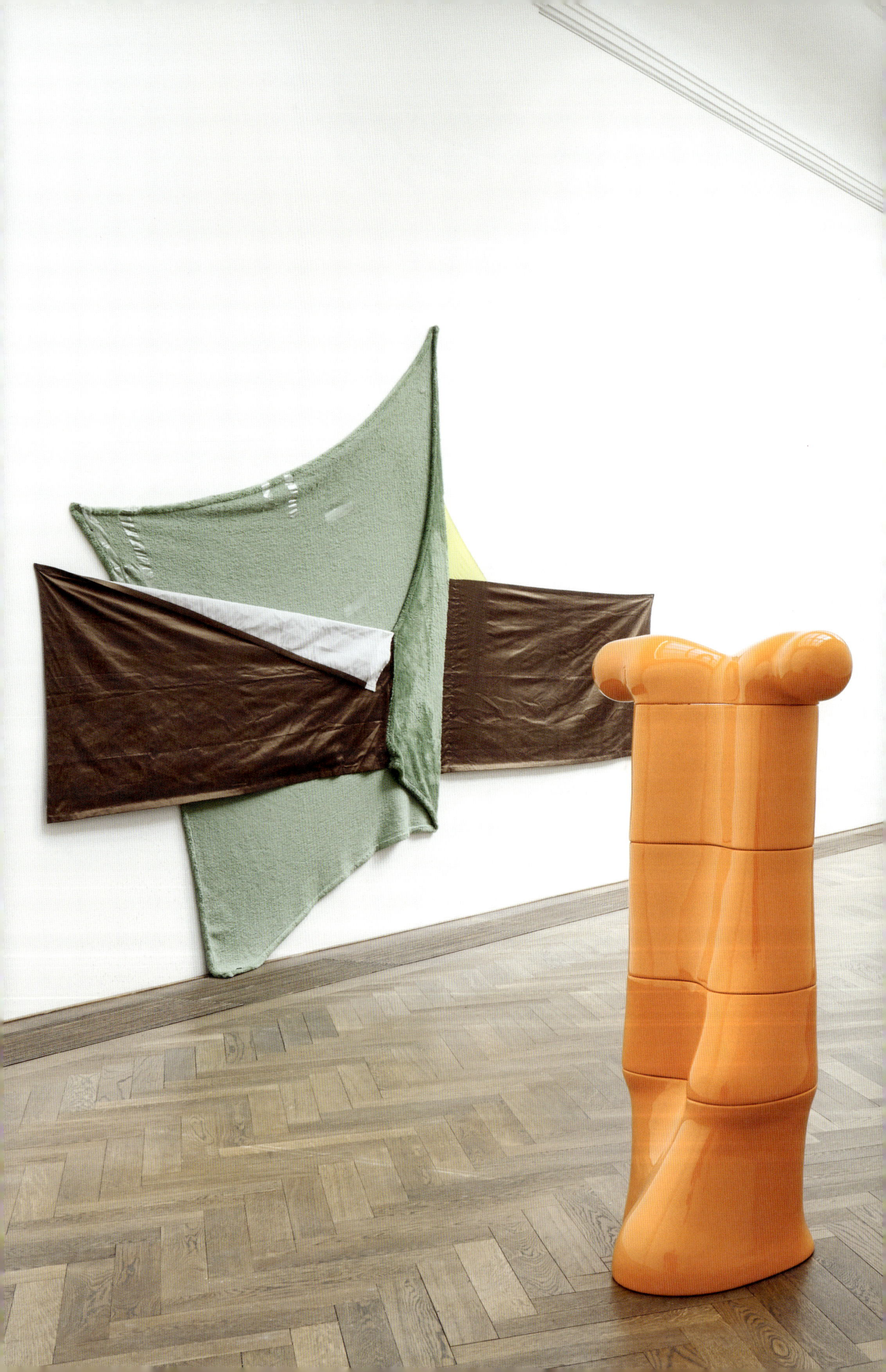

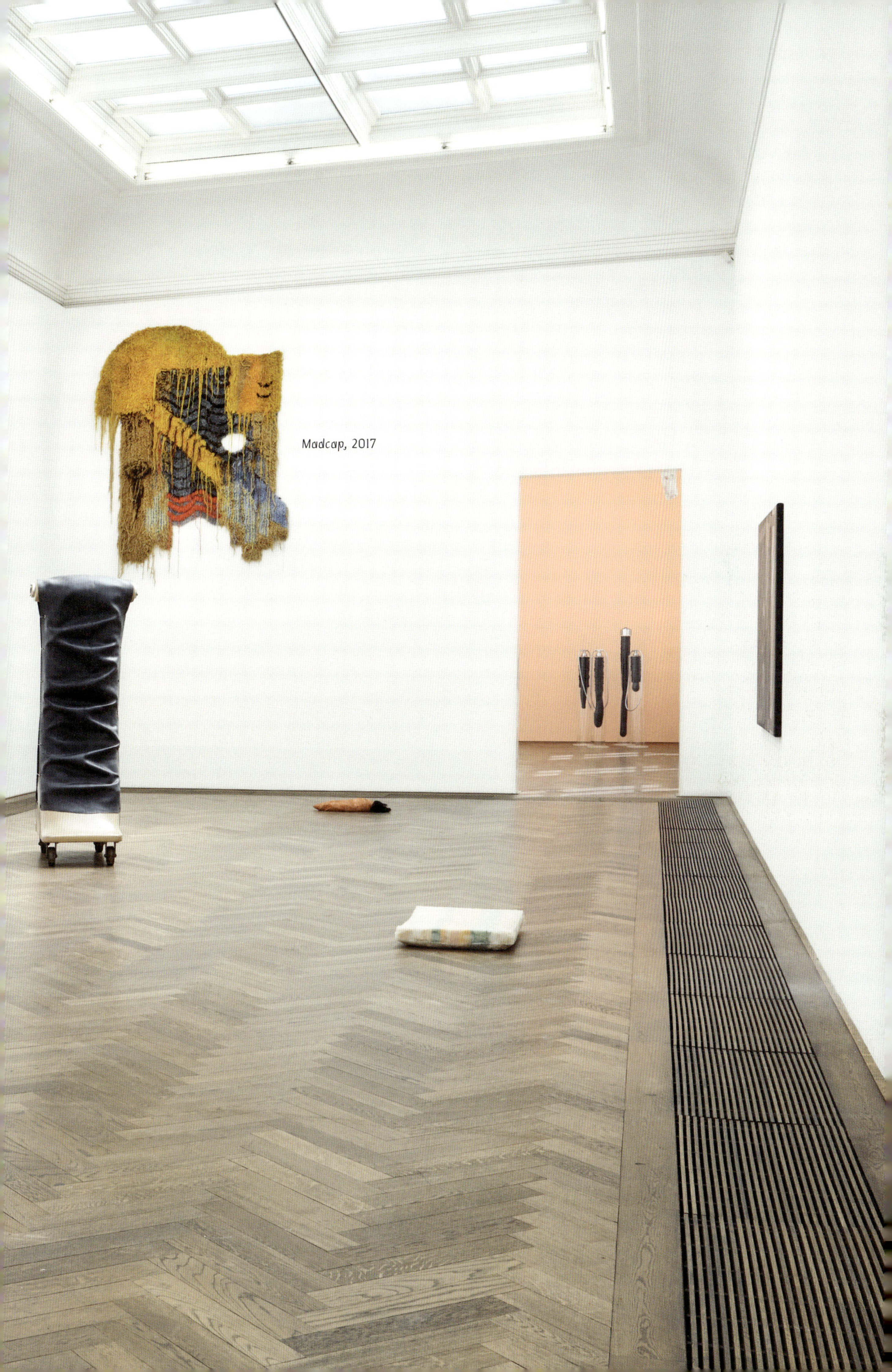

Madcap, 2017

A.O.O., 2017

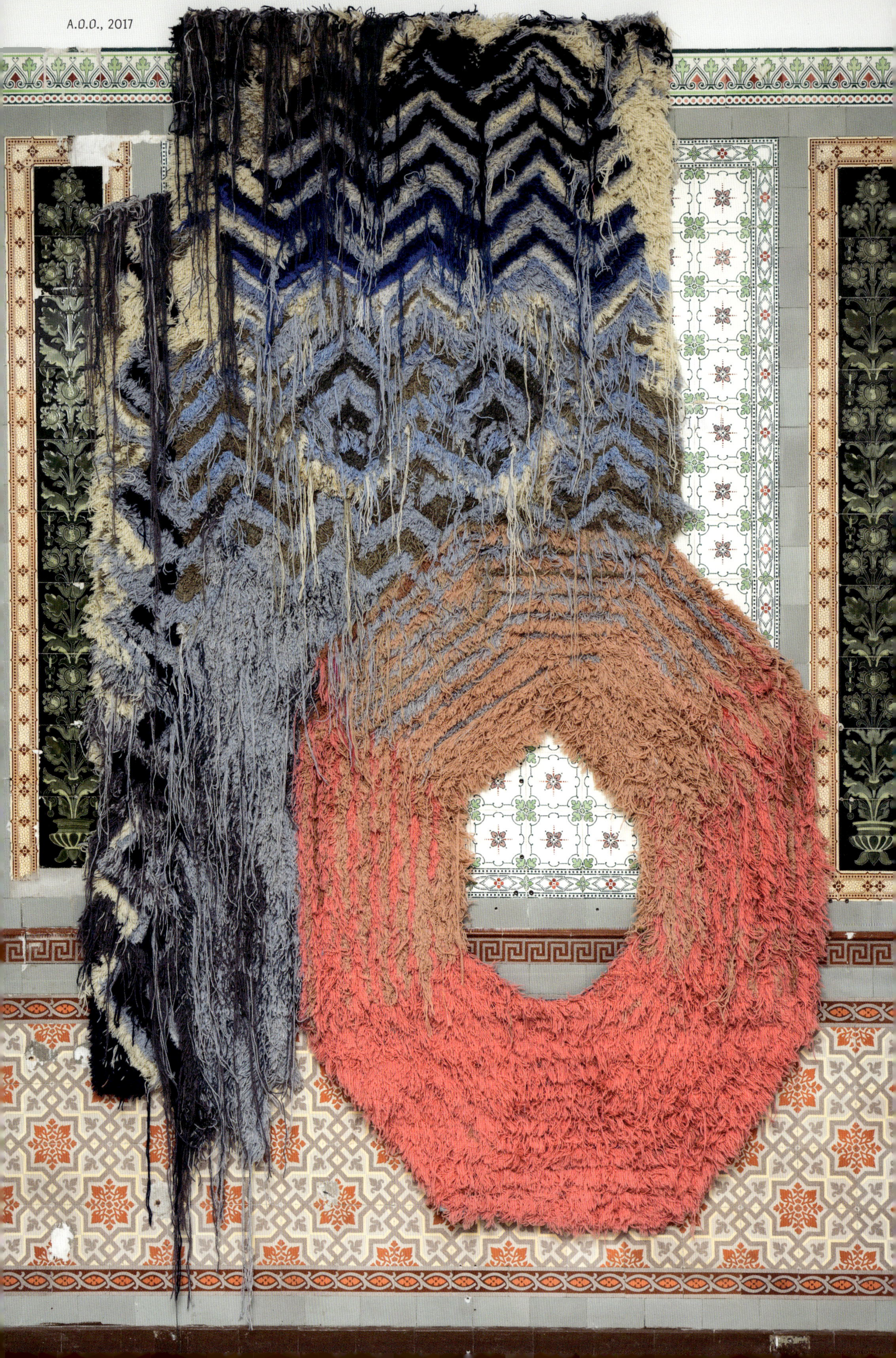

Biography

Caroline Achaintre
Born 1969 in Toulouse, FR
Lives and works in London, UK

Education

2001–2003
Postgraduate studies, Fine Art, Goldsmiths College, London, UK

1998–2000
Undergraduate studies, Fine Art, Chelsea College of Art & Design, London, UK

1996–1998
Undergraduate studies, Fine Art, Kunsthochschule in Halle/Saale, DE

1991–1996
Apprenticeship and work as blacksmith artist, Zirndorf and Berlin, DE

Solo Exhibitions

2018
Dissolver, Dortmunder Kunstverein, Dortmund, DE
Wimper, Touchstones Rochdale, Rochdale, UK
Duo Infernal, Art: Concept, Paris, FR
Fantômas, De La Warr Pavilion, Bexhill on Sea, UK, & BE-PART, Waregem, BE

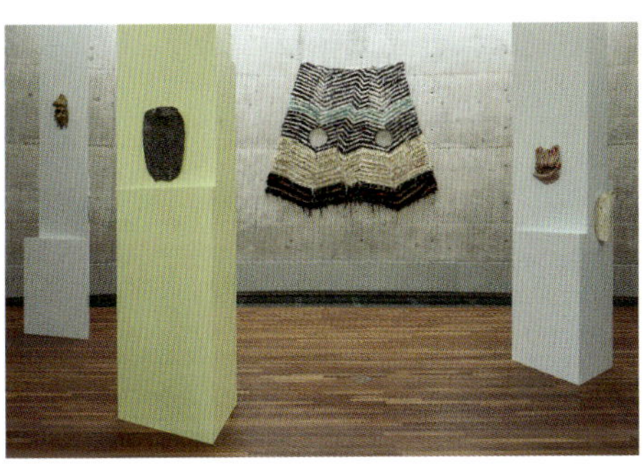

Cape Count, 2018

2017
Escáner: Caroline Achaintre, Museo de Arte Precolombino Casa del Alabado, Quito, EC
Caroline Achaintre, FRAC Champagne-Ardenne, Reims, FR

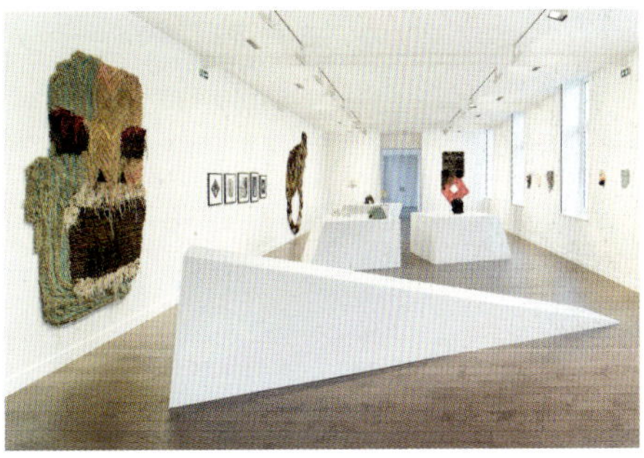

Bfor, 2017

Caroline Achaintre A.O.O., Farbvision, Berlin, DE

2016
Caroline Achaintre, BALTIC Centre for Contemporary Art, Gateshead, UK
Boo, c-o-m-p-o-s-i-t-e, Brussels, BE
Limbo, Arcade, London, UK

2015
Caroline Achaintre, Art Now, Tate Britain, London, UK

2014
Present/Future, Illy Prize, Castello di Rivoli, Turin, IT
Mooner, Arcade, London, UK

2013
Camp Coo, UH Galleries, Hertfordshire, UK

2012
Trip-Dip, Arcade, London, UK

2010
Couleur Locale, Arcade, London, UK

2008
Novelty, Mirko Mayer Galerie, Cologne, DE
Visor Visitor, Fake Estate, New York, US

2007
Six Strings, Blow de la Barra, London, UK

2006
Caroline Achaintre, Mirko Mayer Galerie, Cologne, DE

2005
DEEDIE, The Showroom, London, UK

2004
Caroline Achaintre, Lawrence O'Hana Gallery, London, UK
Caroline Achaintre, Mirko Mayer Galerie, Cologne, DE
QUARTERS, Whitechapel Project Space, London, UK

2002
Billboard, Mafuji Gallery, London, UK

2001
Kampagne, Kunstverein Kohlenhof Nuremberg, DE

Selected Group Exhibitions

2018
Pissing in the River. Again!, Kunstraum Kreuzberg/Bethanien, Berlin, DE
Childhood: Another Banana Day for the Perfect Fish, Palais de Tokyo, Paris, FR

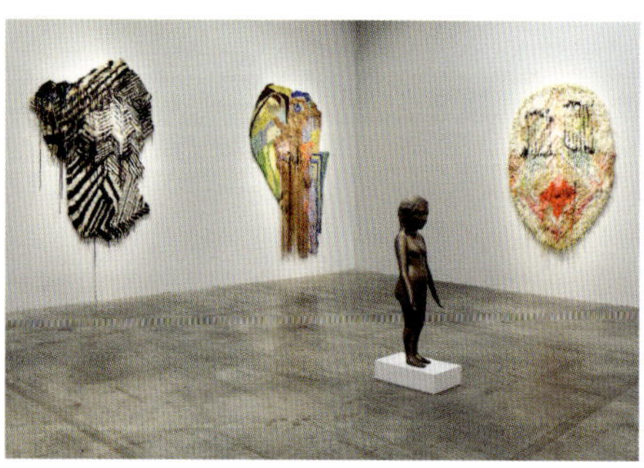

N.O.C., *Todo Custo*, *Cornelia*, 2018

DRAF x MOSTYN: She sees the shadows, MOSTYN, Llandudno, Wales, UK
Baltic Triennial 13 – Give up the Ghost, Contemporary Art Centre, Vilnius, LT
A Forest, Arcade, London, UK
Nomadic Murals: Contemporary Tapestries and Carpets, BOCA Museum, Miami, US
TERRA – A contemporary history of clay, Hotel Contemporary, London, UK

2017
En Crue, Fondation Albert Gleizes, Lyon, FR
Morphogenesis, Galeria Francisco Fino, Lisbon, PT
Ungestalt, Kunsthalle Basel, Basel, CH
Entangled: Threads and Making, Turner Contemporary, Margate, UK
Pre-Capital, La Panacée, Montpellier, FR

2016
XXXmASS, Kate Werble Gallery, New York, US
A Conversation About Ceramics, Galleria Monica de Cardenas, Milan, IT
Making & Unmaking, Camden Arts Centre, London, UK

2015
Folleree & Folleroo, Arcade, London, UK
The British Art Show 8, touring exhibition, Leeds, Edinburgh, Norwich, Southampton, UK

2014
Deep One Perfect Morning, Kerlin Gallery, Dublin, IE
Vernacular Alchemists, Centre d'art contemporain Passerelle, Brest, FR
Decorum, The Power Station of Art, Shanghai, CN
More Material, Salon 94, New York, US
Accordion, Laura Bartlett Gallery, London, UK

2013
A-Tri-Lick, Peer, London, UK
Decorum, Musée d'Art Moderne de la Ville de Paris, Paris, FR
The Hecklers, The New Art Gallery Walsall, Walsall, UK
Six Possibilities for a Sculpture, La Loge, Brussels, BE
Are You Alright? New Art From Britain, MOCCA, Toronto, CA

2012
La Demeure Joyeuse, Galerie Francesca Pia, Zurich, CH
The London Open, Whitechapel Gallery, London, UK
Whitewashing the Moon, Project Arts Centre, Dublin, IE

Bouvard et Pécuchet's Compendious Quest for Beauty, DRAF, London, UK
Caroline Achaintre, Sara Barker, Alice Channer, Eastside Projects, Birmingham, UK
Mocha Non-Truth, Cul De Sac Gallery, London, UK
James Tower and Contemporary Ceramic Art, Gimpel Fils, London, UK
Laying down and kissing the love in the mist, Kendall Koppe Gallery, Glasgow, UK

2011
Slipped, Wysing Arts Centre, Cambridge, UK
Imagine Being Here Now, The 6th Momentum Biennial, Moss, NO
Adventures in a Miniature Landscape, Log, Bergamo, IT

2010
Collision, Museum of Art, Rhode Island School of Design, Providence, US
Newspeak: British Art Now, Saatchi Gallery, London, UK
Das Vertraute Unvertraute, Württembergischer Kunstverein, Stuttgart, DE

2009
Free Radicals, Arcade, London, UK
Cabinet Afrique, Cell Project Space, London, UK

2008
Blue Balls, APF LAB, New York, US
Soft Spot, 0047, Oslo, NO

2007
Behemoth, Danielle Arnaud Gallery, London, UK
Amongst the Ashes and Millionaires, Ancient & Modern, London, UK

2006
Until it Makes Sense, Galerie Thaddaeus Ropac, Paris, FR, and Seventeen, London, UK
Good Vibrations, Palazzo delle Papesse, Siena, IT
If it didn't exist you'd have to invent it: a partial Showroom history, The Showroom, London, UK

2005
Acid Rain, Glassbox/Galerie Michel Rein, Paris, FR
Brief Encounter, The Reykjavík Academy, Reykjavík, IS
Transfer, m-projects, Cologne, DE

Residencies

2017
Fondation Albert Gleizes, Sablons, FR

2015
AIT, Tokyo, JP

2014
Camden Arts Centre, London, UK

Scholarships and Awards

2013
Present/Future, Illy Prize, Artissima, Turin, IT

2007
British Council, Travel Grant for New York, US

2006
Arts Council, Grant for Individual Artists
British Council, Travel Grant for Reykjavík, IS

2004
Arts Council, Grant for Individual Artists
Elephants Trust, Grant for Individual Artists

2003
British Council, Travel Grant for Tirana, AL

1998
DAAD German Academic Exchange Service scholarship to take up postgraduate studies in London, UK
kunstpreis 98, award and exhibition, Kreissparkasse Koethen, DE

Public Collections

FRAC Aquitaine, Bordeaux, FR
FRAC Champagne-Ardenne, Reims, FR

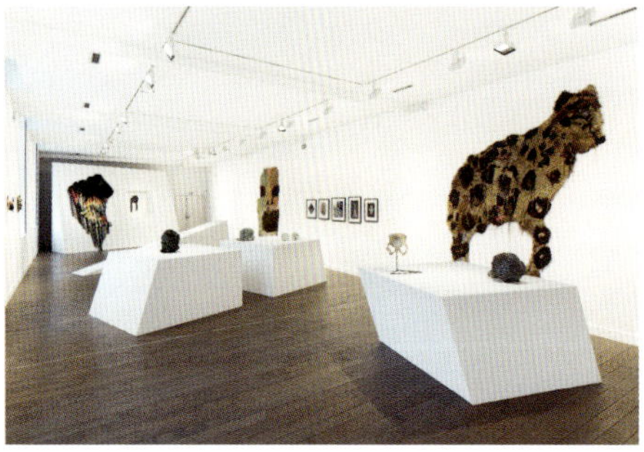

Beasts's Beast, 2017

Arts Council Collection, London, UK
DRAF, London, UK
Musée d'Art Moderne de la Ville de Paris, Paris, FR
Saatchi Gallery, London, UK
Tate Collection, London, UK
University of Hertfordshire Galleries, Hatfield, UK
Southampton City Art Gallery & Museum, Southampton, UK

Catalogues

Caroline Achaintre, BALTIC Centre for Contemporary Art, Gateshead, and FRAC Champagne-Ardenne, Reims, 2016.
Authors Anne Dressen, Zoe Gray, Emma Dean.

Dissolver, Dortmunder Kunstverein, 2018.
Author Oriane Durand.

Escáner, Museo de Arte Precolombino Casa del Alabado, 2017.
Authors Manuela Moscoso, Manuela Ribadeneira, Pablo Lafuente.

Phoon, 2017

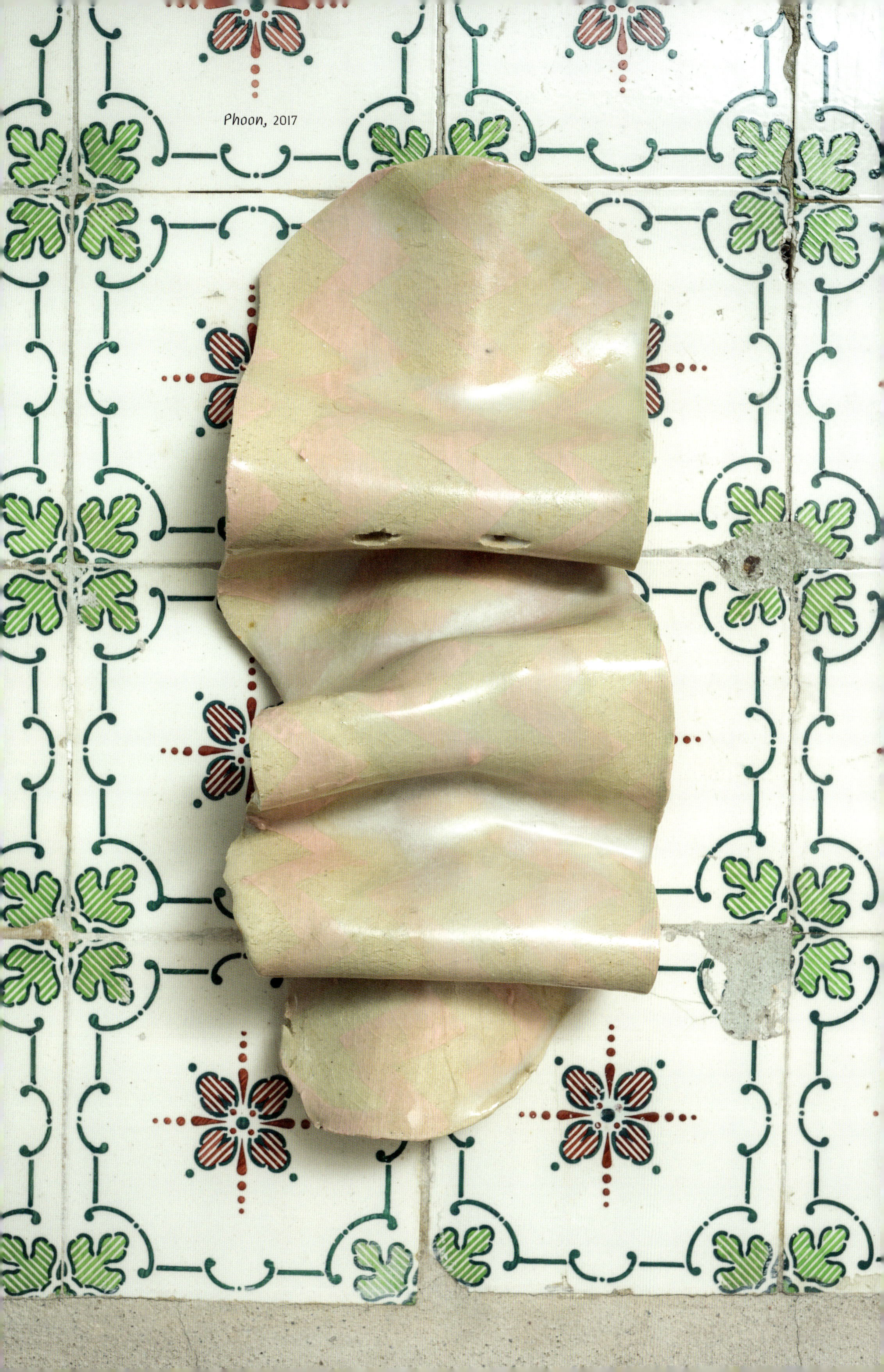

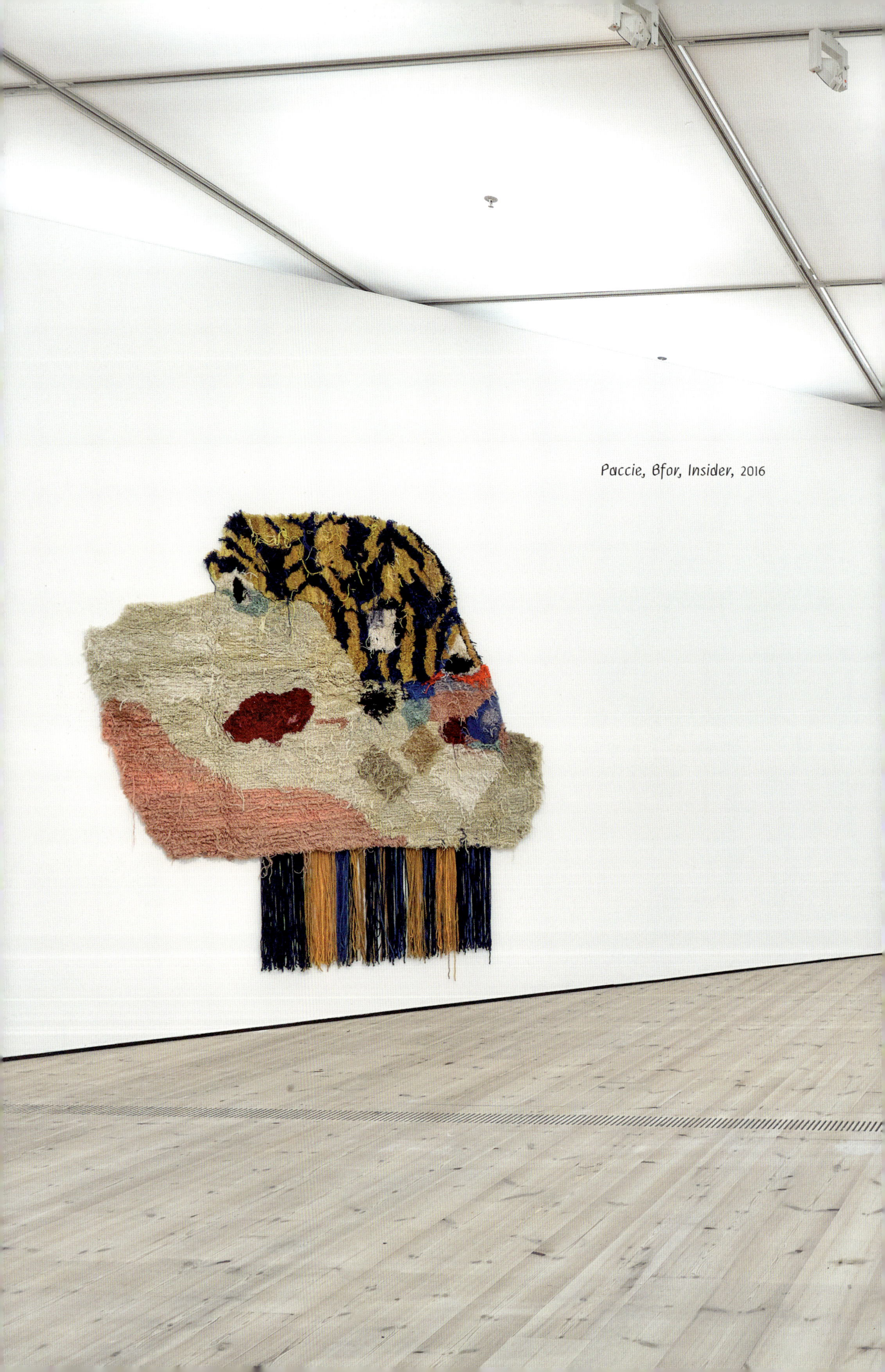

Paccie, Bfor, Insider, 2016

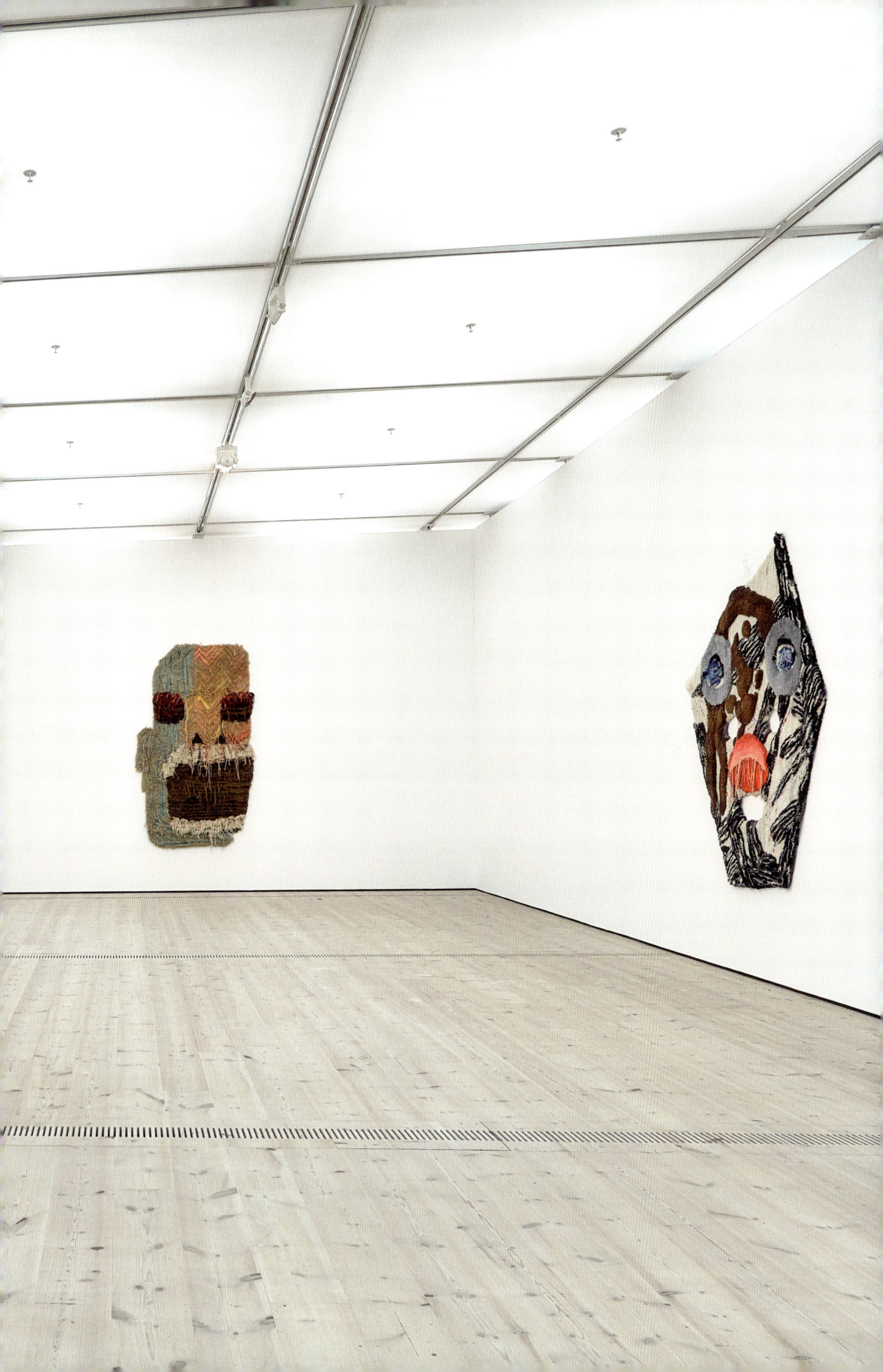

List of Works

Ray Gun, 2017
Watercolor and ink on paper,
33.8 × 24 cm

Space Pup, 2017
Watercolor and ink on paper,
31.5 × 38 cm

Licker, 2019
Ceramic, 46 × 27 cm

Re-Wine, 2019
Ceramic, 55 × 24 cm

Scanner, 2018
Watercolor and ink on paper,
37 × 27 cm

Tenpence, 2019
Ceramic, 47.5 × 34 cm

Cruizer, 2019
Tapestry, hand-tufted wool,
256 × 220 cm

Autobahn, 2013
Watercolor and ink on paper,
34 × 26 cm

El Ouster, 2019
Ceramic, 38 × 22.5 cm

Tatter, 2019
Ceramic, 45 × 30 cm

Monika, 2019
Ceramic, 40 × 28 cm

Glover, 2018
Tapestry, hand-tufted wool,
170 × 190 cm

Ernest, 2019
Ceramic, 45 × 34 cm

Oing Oings, 2016
Watercolor and ink on paper,
31 × 25 cm

Sir Plus, 2019
Ceramic, 92 × 34 cm

Ashlar, 2019
Ceramic, 57 × 32 cm

Brunco, 2019
Tapestry, hand-tufted wool,
240 × 165 cm

Borg, 2019
Ceramic, 51 × 40 cm

Be-Motz, 2019
Ceramic, 47 × 23 cm

Super-Vette, 2019
Ceramic, 103 × 36 cm

Oorrn, 2019
Ceramic, 68 × 32 cm

Akin, 2019
Ceramic, 71.5 × 34 cm

Chris P., 2019
Ceramic, 39 × 31 cm

Copy-Cat, 2019
Watercolor and ink on paper,
37 × 25.5 cm

Meute II, 2019
Leather, pins, 65 × 40 × 38 cm

Martha, 2019
Ceramic, 32 × 20.5 cm

Trunkk P., 2018
Ceramic, 53 × 32 × 30 cm
Photo by Simon Vogel

Wimper, 2018
Watercolor and ink on paper,
31.5 × 38 cm

Mart'an G'rl, 2019
Tapestry, hand-tufted wool,
235 × 200 cm

Image Credits

p. 10
Rock, 2000
Artist's own

p. 14
Frank, 2013

p. 15
Double-Dealing, 2005
Artist's own

p. 18
Ray-Inn, 2010

p. 19
Wanderer, 2012

p. 22
Skwash, 2014

p. 24
Astra Y, 2014

p. 72
Monmec, 2017

pp. 74–75
Madcap, in Ungestalt, Kunsthalle Basel, Basel, 2017
Works from left and right:
Eric N. Mack, Joachim Bandau, Caroline Achaintre, Liz Magor, Michaela Eichwald
Photo by Philipp Hänger

p. 76
A.O.O., in A.D.O., Farbvision, Berlin, 2017
Photo by Florian Balze

p. 77
Cape Count, in Fantômas, Be-Part, Waregem, 2018
Photo by Dirk Pauwels

p. 77
Bfor, in Caroline Achaintre, FRAC Champagne-Ardenne, Reims, 2017
Photo by Martin Argyoglo

p. 78
N.O.C., *Todo Custo*, *Cornelia*, in Childhood: Another Banana Day for the Perfect Fish, Palais de Tokyo, Paris, 2018
Bronze sculpture in image by Kiki Smith
Photo by Aurélien Mole

p. 80
Beasts's Beast, in Caroline Achaintre, FRAC Champagne-Ardenne, Reims, 2017
Photo by Martin Argyoglo

p. 81
Phoon, in A.D.O., Farbvision, Berlin, 2017
Photo by Florian Balze

pp. 82–83
Paccie, *Bfor*, *Insider*, in BALTIC Centre for Contemporary Art, Gateshead, 2016
Photo by John McKenzie

All works courtesy of the artist, Arcade London & Art:Concept Paris. Photography by Andy Keate, unless otherwise stated. If in spite of our thorough research any individual illustrations have not been correctly attributed or acknowledged, we offer our apologies and would appreciate any information that will allow us to rectify the matter in future editions.

Authors

Charlotte Cosson & Emmanuelle Luciani are art historians and curators. They recently curated *COOL – As a State of Mind* at MAMO (Marseille), *From Transhuman to South Perspectives* at Rowing (London), *DOMESTIC – Like Pre-Raphaelite Brotherhood* at Truth and Consequences (Geneva), and *Pre-capital: Popular and Rural Forms in Contemporary Art* at La Panacée – MoCo (Montpellier) with Nicolas Bourriaud. They are running *CODE South Way* magazine and founded South Way Studio, a residency where international artists are invited to theorize and produce in dialogue with them in Marseille. Their methodology is Oracular / Vernacular: they are sourcing material in history in order to project anew toward the future, and they do not conceive to think without producing. Influenced by Heinrich Wölfflin, Alois Riegl, and Walter Benjamin, they consider art as the formal crystallization of societal changes. In 2018 they were nominated for the AICA prize and started to teach at the Paris Institute of Political Studies (Sciences Po). In summer 2019 they are theorizing the way out of capitals from the nineteenth century in a double exhibition at MRAC (Sérignan) and l'Abbaye de Fontfroide.

Oriane Durand is artistic director of the Dortmunder Kunstverein. She studied art history at the Sorbonne in Paris and the FU Berlin. She repositioned the Dortmunder Kunstverein with solo exhibitions by Sol Calero, Elaine Cameron-Weir, and Caroline Achaintre, as well as group exhibitions such as *Picknick am Wegesrand*, *Hunger*, and *Bamboo Bar at the Edge of the Universe*, which examine our technology-driven, globalized society and in particular the construction of futuristic scenarios. From 2010 to 2014, she was curator of the Kunstverein Nürnberg. In 2014 Oriane Durand joined the Bonner Kunstverein, where she invited Klaus Merkel, Raphaela Vogel, and Jonathan Binet for solo exhibitions. As an author, she contributes her writing regularly to various publications.

Stella Rollig has been CEO and Artistic Director of the Belvedere since January 2017. She studied German and Art History at the University of Vienna and later worked as an arts journalist (for ORF, *Der Standard* and others). From 1994 to 1996 Rollig was the Austrian Federal Curator for the Fine Arts; during this time she also founded *Depot, Kunst und Diskussion* at MuseumsQuartier Wien. From 2004 to 2016 she was Artistic Director of the LENTOS art museum in Linz and from 2011 also Director of NORDICO Stadtmuseum Linz. In addition to her curatorial roles, Rollig has taught at numerous institutions.

Autorinnen

Charlotte Cosson & Emmanuelle Luciani sind Kunsthistorikerinnen und Kuratorinnen. Zuletzt kuratierten sie COOL – *As a State of Mind*, MAMO (Marseille), *From Transhuman to South Perspectives*, Rowing (London), *DOMESTIC – Like Pre-Raphaelite Brotherhood*, Truth and Consequences (Genf), und *Pre-capital: Popular and Rural Forms in Contemporary Art*, La Panacée – MoCo (Montpellier) mit Nicolas Bourriaud. Sie geben die Zeitschrift CODE South Way heraus und gründeten das South Way Studio, ein Residency-Programm in Marseille, das internationale Künstlerinnen und Künstler einlädt, im Dialog mit ihnen zu theoretisieren und zu produzieren. Ihre Methode bezeichnen sie als *Oracular/Vernacular*: Sie suchen in der Geschichte nach Materialien, um damit für die Zukunft zu planen; in ihrer Vorstellung sind Denken und Produzieren nicht voneinander zu trennen. In Anlehnung an Heinrich Wölfflin, Alois Riegl und Walter Benjamin betrachten sie Kunst als eine formale Kristallisation gesellschaftlichen Wandels. 2018 waren sie für den AICA-Preis nominiert und begannen, am Pariser Institut d'études politiques (Sciences Po) zu unterrichten. Im Sommer 2019 entwickeln sie in einer Doppelausstellung im MRAC (Sérignan) und in der Abbaye de Fontfroide eine Theorie über den Auszug aus den Kapitalen des 19. Jahrhunderts.

Oriane Durand ist künstlerische Leiterin des Dortmunder Kunstvereins. Sie hat Kunstgeschichte an der Sorbonne in Paris und der FU Berlin studiert. Mit Einzelausstellungen von Sol Calero, Elaine Cameron-Weir und Caroline Achaintre, aber auch Gruppenausstellungen wie *Picknick am Wegesrand*, *Hunger* und *Bamboo Bar at the Edge of the Universe*, die sich mit unserer technisierten, globalisierten Gesellschaft und insbesondere der Konstruktion futuristischer Szenarien auseinandersetzen, verlieh sie dem Dortmunder Kunstverein eine neue Positionierung. Von 2010 bis 2014 war sie im Kunstverein Nürnberg als Kuratorin tätig. 2014 wechselte Oriane Durand zum Bonner Kunstverein, wo sie Klaus Merkel, Raphaela Vogel oder Jonathan Binet für Einzelausstellungen einlud. Als Autorin schreibt sie regelmäßig Beiträge für Publikationen.

Stella Rollig ist seit Jänner 2017 Generaldirektorin und wissenschaftliche Geschäftsführerin des Belvedere. Sie studierte Germanistik und Kunstgeschichte an der Universität Wien und war als Kunstpublizistin tätig (unter anderem ORF, *Der Standard*). Von 1994 bis 1996 war Stella Rollig österreichische Bundeskuratorin für bildende Kunst, in dieser Zeit gründete sie auch *Depot. Kunst und Diskussion* im MuseumsQuartier Wien. Von 2004 bis 2016 leitete die Ausstellungsmacherin das LENTOS Kunstmuseum Linz, ab 2011 zusätzlich das NORDICO Stadtmuseum Linz. Neben ihrer kuratorischen Tätigkeit lehrte Stella Rollig an zahlreichen Institutionen.

This catalogue is published on the occasion of the exhibition *Caroline Achaintre. Dauerwelle / Permanent Wave*, May 17 to September 15, 2019 at the Belvedere 21, Vienna.

Artistic Director, CEO:
Stella Rollig

CFO:
Wolfgang Bergmann

Curator of the Exhibition:
Stella Rollig

Curatorial Assistant:
Johanna Hofer

Exhibition Management and Loans:
Stephan Pumberger

Exhibition Production:
Tanja Angermann-Cekinmez
Sibylle Reichmann

Exhibitions & Programs:
Harald Krejci

Education:
Susanne Wögerbauer
Michaela Höß

Marketing:
Markus Wiesenhofer

Visitor Services:
Margarete Stechl

Communications & Digital Belvedere:
Monika Voglgruber
Irene Jäger

Research Center:
Christian Huemer

Conservation Department:
Stefanie Jahn

Belvedere
Prinz Eugen-Straße 27
1030 Vienna
www.belvedere.at

belvedere 21

Publication

Editor:
Stella Rollig

Authors:
Charlotte Cosson
Emmanuelle Luciani
Oriane Durand
Stella Rollig

Graphic Design:
Fraser Muggeridge studio

Publication Management:
Eva Lahnsteiner

Copy Editing (German):
Katharina Sacken

Copy Editing (English):
Keonaona Peterson, Sam Osborn

Translation (German–English):
Laura Freeburn

Translation (English–German):
Barbara Hess

Picture Editing:
Pixelstorm, Vienna

Printed and bound by:
gugler GmbH, Melk

Published by:
VfmK Verlag für moderne Kunst GmbH
Salmgasse 4a
A-1030 Vienna
hello@vfmk.org
www.vfmk.org

VERLAG FÜR MODERNE KUNST

Distribution
Europe: LKG, www.lkg-va.de
UK: Cornerhouse Publications, www.cornerhousepublications.org
USA: D.A.P., www.artbook.com

Bibliographic information published by Die Deutsche Nationalbibliothek

Die Deutsche Bibliothek lists this publication in the Deutsche Nationalbibliografie; detailed bibliographic data is available in the Internet at: www.dnb.de.

ISBN 978-3-903114-82-1 (museum edition)
ISBN 978-3-903269-95-8 (trade edition)

All rights reserved
Printed in Austria

© 2019 Belvedere, Vienna, Verlag für moderne Kunst, the artists, and the authors